AF364604

Changing history to HERstory

Based on the ground-breaking and uplifting art exhibition
by Kat Shaw, highlighting the amazing women who
have walked before us and changed the world.

Written and illustrated by Kat Shaw

Girl God Books

Copyright 2021
All Rights Reserved

ISBN 9788293725251

All illustrations are the property of Kat Shaw. All rights reserved. None of the
illustrations may be reproduced or utilized in any form or by any means, electronic or
mechanical, including photocopying, recording or by any information storage and
retrieval system, without prior written permission from Kat Shaw.

www.thegirlgod.com

Girl God Books

Mentorship with Goddess: Growing Sacred Womanhood
Mentorship with Goddess is a workbook – a year-long programme – a rite of passage –
especially useful for the transition into autonomous adulthood – and also for the menopause
journey. The programme can be undertaken solo or as a group. The specific aim is growing Sacred
Womanhood. Mentorship with Goddess is an embodied education and evolution, which combines
metacognition, intuition, and instinct. It is principally about discovering, accepting, and loving
yourself, and simultaneously protecting and vulnerably showing up as your whole Self in the world.

Rainbow Goddess: Celebrating Neurodiversity
Rainbow Goddess lives within the full spectrum of the human mind. There is not one way of
thinking, learning, or behaving that she does not inhabit fully and sanctify. This carnival and
inclusive Goddess celebrates the gifts of those whose minds exist and operate outside the box
of society's 'norms' – and she trumpets the creativity, visions, and uniqueness of these humans.
Rainbow Goddess protectively arcs around those who encounter the struggles of patriarchal
expectation and judgement of neurodiverse women. This Girl God anthology showcases the voices
and art of women as they express their experiences of neurodiversity. It is a thanksgiving for the
creativity, imagination, self-awareness, super-power sensitivity, problem-solving, planning abilities,
resilience, and new ways of seeing the world that these women offer.

The Crone Initiation: Women Speak on the Menopause Journey
The Crone Initiation is an anthology of women's experiences of perimenopause and
menopause, and the part Goddess plays in this journey. Crone's presence in the breakdowns
and breakthroughs, the disintegration and rebuilding, is expressed through words and art.
Meaning is reclaimed and the power of the Elder restored.

Willendorf's Legacy: The Sacred Body
Travel through time and discover a world where the fullness of women was both admired and
deified. Reclaim your beautiful Goddess body through the rich pages of this powerful collection of
art, poetry and essays celebrating our divine inheritance as daughters of Willendorf.

In Defiance of Oppression - The Legacy of Boudicca
In Defiance of Oppression - The Legacy of Boudica is an anthology that encapsulates the Spirit of
the defiant warrior in a modern apathetic age. No longer will the voices of our sisters go unheard,
as the ancient Goddesses return to the battlements, calling to ignite the spark within each and
every one of us—to defy oppression wherever we find it, and stand together in solidarity. Delve
into the pages and remember the spirit of defiance within you. We are still here, we are standing
with you, and we shall never, ever, give up.

Warrior Queen: Answering the Call of The Morrigan
Warrior Queen: Answering the Call of The Morrigan is a powerful anthology about the Irish Celtic
Goddess. Each contributor brings The Morrigan to life with unique stories that invite readers to
partake and inspire them to pen their own. Included are essays, poems, stories, chants, rituals, and
art from dozens of story-tellers and artists from around the world, illustrating and recounting the
many ways this powerful Goddess of war, death, and prophecy has changed their lives.

www.thegirlgod.com

Additional Offerings by Kat Shaw

I am a Goddess: Colour Your Way to Self-Love
Join Kat Shaw on the path to self-love through each page of this unique and uplifting colouring book. You will embark upon your journey of empowerment and creativity - embraced within the unconditionally loving arms of Goddess.

Walking the Path of Kali
This book aims to lead you, through walking your own path, around the wheel of Kali throughout the year, and establishing a direct and individual connection with Her – whilst remembering that She is and always has been within us all

The Path of Kali Oracle
A set of 54 cards containing 18 archetype cards, 18 affirmation cards and 18 symbol cards along with 18 corresponding crystals to guide you, empower you, offer insights and impart wisdom into your soul from the very essence of Kali. This deck facilitates integration of Kali's teachings into your life by feeling, knowing and walking alongside Her 18 archetypes.

Volume 1&2: The Path of the Divine Feminine Empowering Goddess Oracle Cards
Each volume includes a set of 60 stunning oracle cards, painted and written with love. These glorious oracle decks will enable you to step into the incredible teachings, healing, wisdom and adoration of the Goddess in her many, many faces as She awakens your soul and brings magic and empowerment into your life.

Imperfectly Fabulous Empowering Affirmation Cards for the 21st Century Goddess
A set of 75 inspirational cards, painted and written with love. These cards will empower your soul as you rise and awaken your inner Goddess – stepping into the Divine Feminine who resides inside the glorious woman that you are – totally in your own skin, loving, powerful, strong and full of magic – embracing your fabulous imperfections and owning your magnificence exactly as you are meant to be.

And Still I Rise
A book based on the inspirational exhibition by Kat Shaw featuring 85 glorious women who have survived, and used the broken pieces of their lives to build a bridge and walk with power.
Coming soon!

Prints, canvasses, cards, original paintings and merchandise are also available at the KatShawArtist Etsy shop: Www.Etsy.com/uk/shop/KatShawArtist

katshaw.art

Dedicated to my wonderfully strong daughter -
who will change the world.

These strong and influential women have changed the world in such a huge and impactful way – yet, the majority of them have gone unnoticed. Now is the time to honour the women who have walked before us and changed history to HERstory. These women (and the many others I have not mentioned) may not have intentionally set out to become role models but have all achieved extraordinarily amazing things by following their hearts, talents, dreams, beliefs and passions. They didn't listen to the confining drone of a society that places women in the "cannot do that" box – they dared, and they took a stand, stepping into their power, following their truth and using their voices to be different and make a change to the world we live in today. We are standing on their shoulders. We are using the stones thrown at them as women to build our paths forwards. They are the women who walked before us. It's time to honour them now.

It's time to change history to HERstory.

Table of Contents

37 Andrea Dworkin: "In her life she is the proof of woman's capacity and will to survive."

38 Dion Fortune: "A religion without a Goddess is halfway to atheism."

39 Judy Chicago: "And then all will live in harmony with each other and the earth."

40 Harriet Tubman: "Every great dream begins with a dreamer."

41 Coretta Scott King: "When your heart is right, your mind and body will follow."

42 Diane Ackerman: "I don't want to get to the end of my life and realise I lived just the length of it..."

43 Lydia Ruyle: "How did I find the Goddess? She called me and I listened."

44 Helen Keller: "The most beautiful things must be felt with the heart."

45 Anne Frank: "Whoever is happy will make others happy too."

46 Kate Bush: "I just know that something good is going to happen."

47 Vita Sackville: "Live life fully, live life passionately."

48 Charlotte Brontë: "I would always rather be happy than dignified."

49 Gertrude Ederle: "I just knew that if it could be done, it had to be done, and I did it."

50 Ada Lovelace: "I am in a charming state of confusion."

51 Louise L. Hay: "You have been criticizing yourself for years and it hasn't worked..."

52 Justice Ruth Bader Ginsburg: "My mother told me to be a lady."

53 Nayyirah Waheed: "I am mine before I am anyone else's."

54 Suzanne Valadon: "I found myself, I made myself and I said what I had to say."

55 Rupi Kaur: "I stand on the sacrifices of a million women before me."

"We need to re-read our history or "heresy" (her story).
Because of our fear of "heresy" we have buried our history,
and women's names are buried in history. Their resistance is
ignored, their creative work is not mentioned, except if they
are accepted by powerful patriarchal critics."
-Nawal El Saadawi

Rosa Louise McCauley Parks was born in Tuskegee, Alabama, on February 4, 1913. She was an American activist in the civil rights movement best known for her pivotal role in the Montgomery bus boycott when she refused to give up her seat to a white man on an Alabama bus in 1955. The United States Congress has called her "the first lady of civil rights", "the mother of the freedom movement", and "the woman who stood up for herself and others by sitting down".

Back in the 50s, the rule in Montgomery, Alabama, was that if a bus became full, Black people would have to give up their seats to white passengers. Parks, a leader in the local NAACP and the civil rights movement, iconically refused to give up her seat, and remained quiet and dignified throughout, even though it led to her arrest. Her willingness to disobey the rule helped to spark the Montgomery boycott and other efforts to end segregation in America. The Montgomery Bus Boycott was led by a young Rev. Dr. Martin Luther King Jr., and lasted more than a year – during which time Rosa Parks lost her job. When she first refused to move, she took an important step toward making the lives of Black and white people equal, and over the next half-century, Parks became a nationally recognized symbol of dignity and strength in the struggle to end entrenched racial segregation.

Where she and her husband Raymond Parks lived, their lives were fraught with daily frustrations: Black people could attend only certain (inferior) schools, could drink only from specified water fountains and could borrow books only from the "Black" library, among other restrictions. Rosa had had previous run-ins on buses, and she'd clashed with the same driver 12 years earlier. She stood her ground until he pulled her coat sleeve, enraged, to demand her cooperation. Parks left the bus rather than give in.

But, on Thursday, December 1, 1955, when the 42-year-old Rosa Parks was commuting home from a long day of work at the Montgomery Fair department store by bus, she had had enough. Black residents of Montgomery often avoided municipal buses if possible because they found the policy so demeaning. Nonetheless, 70 percent or more riders on a typical day were Black, and on this day Rosa Parks was one of them.

Segregation was written into law; the front of a Montgomery bus was reserved for white citizens, and the seats behind them for Black citizens, and at one point on the route, a white man had no seat because all the seats in the designated "white" section were taken. So the driver told the riders in the four seats of the first row of the "coloured" section to stand, in effect adding another row to the "white" section. The three others obeyed. Parks did not.

"People always say that I didn't give up my seat because I was tired," wrote Parks in her autobiography, "but that isn't true. I was not tired physically... **No, the only tired I was, was tired of giving in.**" Eventually, two police officers approached the stopped bus, assessed the situation, and placed Parks in custody.

On November 13, 1956, the Supreme Court ruled that bus segregation was unconstitutional; the boycott ended on December 20, a day after the Court's written order arrived in Montgomery. Parks – who had lost her job and experienced harassment all year—became known as "the mother of the Civil Rights movement." But due to the continued harassment and threats in the wake of the boycott, Parks, along with her husband and mother, eventually decided to move to Detroit, where Rosa became an administrative aide in the Detroit office of Congressman John Conyers Jr. in 1965. In 1987, she co-founded the Rosa and Raymond Parks Institute for Self-Development, to serve Detroit's youth.

In the years following her retirement, she travelled to lend her support to Civil Rights events and causes and wrote an autobiography, *Rosa Parks: My Story*. In 1999, Parks was awarded the Congressional Gold Medal, the highest honour the United States bestows on a civilian. When she died at age 92 on October 24, 2005, she became the first woman in the nation's history to lie in honour at the U.S. Capitol.

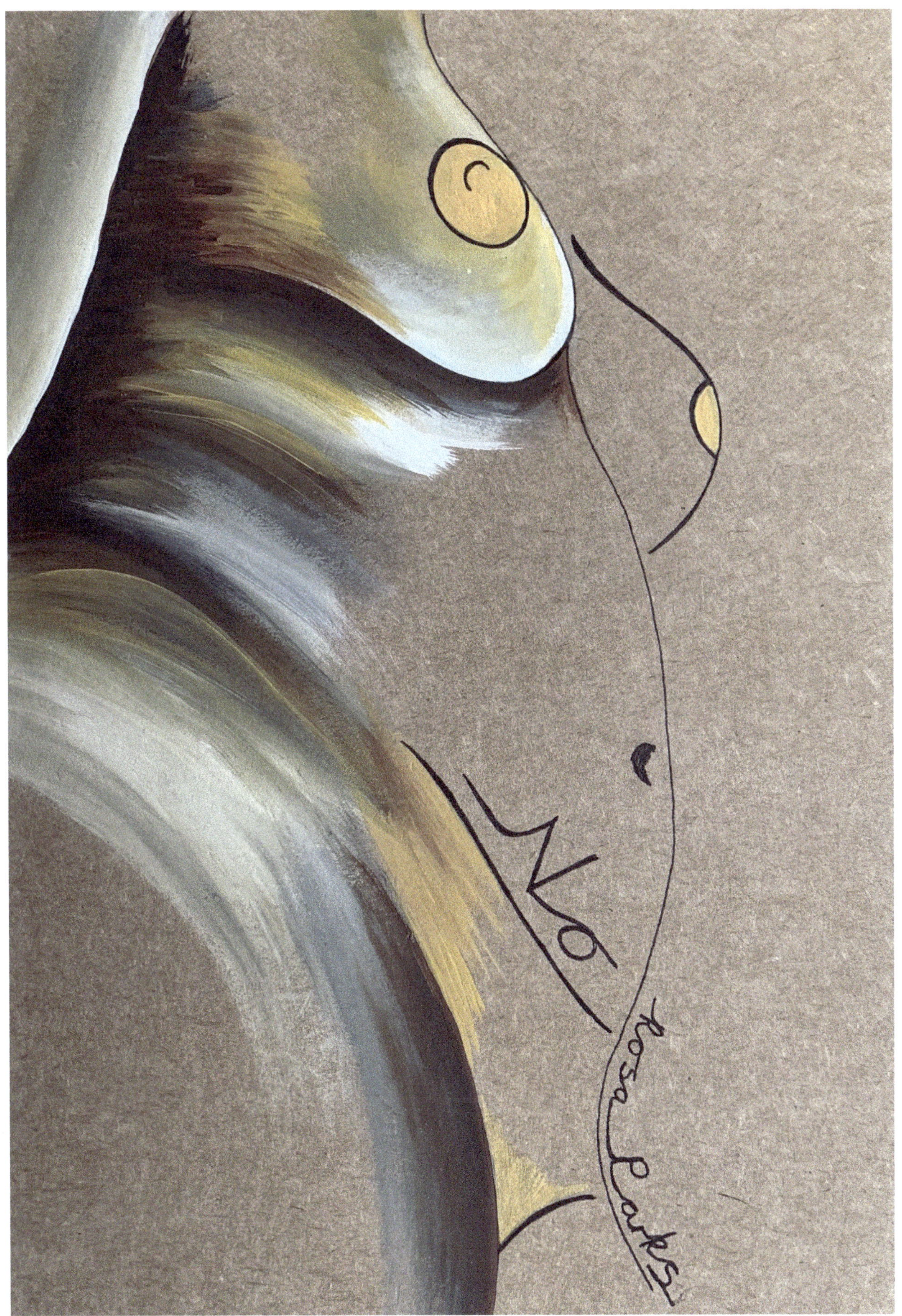
No 9
Rosa Parks

"I am both war and woman and you cannot stop me."

Nikita Gill is a poet and writer. She was brought up in Gurugram, Haryana in India and in her mid-twenties, immigrated to the South of England. She worked as a carer for many years, but says that she has been writing for as long as she can remember. At only 12 years old a non-fiction story she wrote was published in a newspaper in India and she started sharing her poetry on Tumblr almost ten years ago.

Nikita Gill has said that her first manuscript was rejected by 137 publishers, but instead of feeding into unworthiness, becoming disheartened and giving up on her writing, she used the rejection as fuel to better her creative process. Through her perseverance, that certainly happened. She has published many books since then, including *Great Goddesses – Life Lessons from Myths and Monsters*, *Wild Embers – poems of rebellion, fire and beauty* and *Your Soul is a River*. Nikita Gill is a name on the lips of hundreds of thousands of people all over the world who look to her poems for inspiration, hope and empowerment.

Nikita has a very modern view on the ever-changing world of social media and how poetry plays into it, using her platform positively and advocating extremely vocally for poets to be credited as they deserve every time a piece of their work is shared. Having been the victim of famous celebrities like Khloe Kardashian not crediting her work, she has challenged and drawn attention to this, educating people about personal responsibility and ethical sharing within the arts.

In her book *Fierce Fairytales: & Other Stories to Stir Your Soul*, Nikita Gill takes classic tales and turns them upside down with a feminist twist in a way that we have never heard them before. Cinderella turned into the princess who saved herself, Little Red Riding Hood turned into the leader of the wolves to avoid being eaten, and villains turned from nasty creatures into misunderstood characters who could suddenly be related to and seen in a different light.

It is totally amazing to see such a strong woman who is current today, taking on and tackling society, conquering the world and its tired paradigms and inspiring all those along the way who read her poetry.

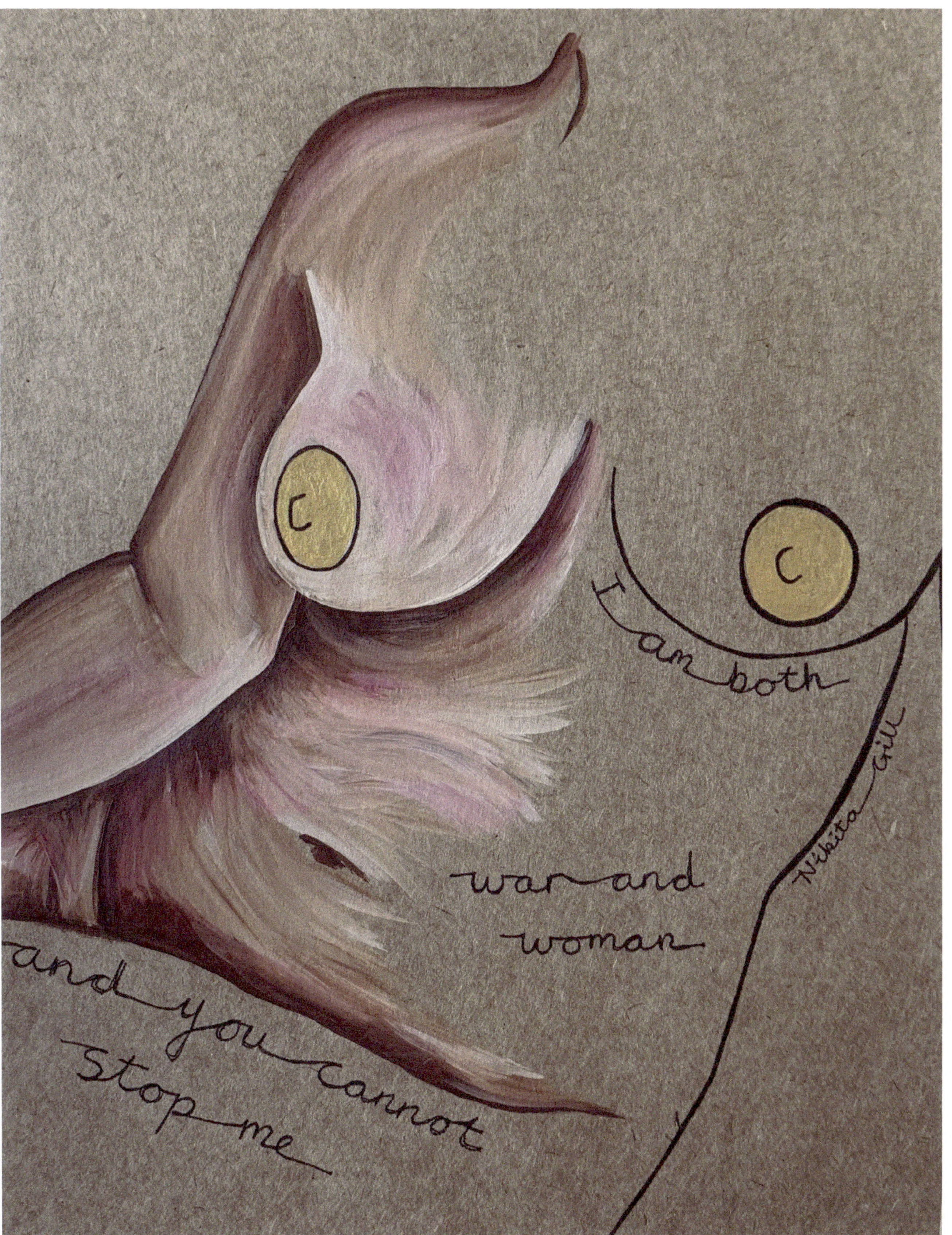

I am both
war and
woman
and you cannot
stop me
Nikita Gill

"Be your own kind of beautiful."

Gabrielle Bonheur "Coco" Chanel (1883 – 1971) was a French fashion designer and business-woman. The founder and namesake of the Chanel brand, she was credited in the post-World War I era with popularizing a sporty, casual chic as the feminine standard of style, replacing the "corseted silhouette" that was dominant beforehand. Coco literally liberated women. By stripping off the constraints of corsets, she unapologetically gave them back their right to breathe and introduced a new, modern style of leveraging bold elegance, which women embraced gladly.

The legendary fashion designer and true icon of style was also a remarkably intelligent and audacious woman. Apart from her creative ingenuity and sharp eye for sophisticated aesthetics, she was an incredibly empowering woman who continues to inspire women of all generations.

More than a century ago, Coco Chanel was a modern woman who challenged stereotypes and conventions, both in fashion and life, and lived by her own rules. Defying conventions and the hypocritical conservatism of the social circles she swiftly moved through, Coco Chanel single-handedly revolutionized the image of the female body by bringing it back to its natural shape and genuine femininity.

Coco Chanel was a woman who wore trousers and smoked in public without any restraint whatsoever, for the simple pleasure of it. Women were inspired by her and reclaimed power over their own bodies, becoming empowered and fighting harder for their rights and an equal position in a patriarchal male-dominated society. Coco Chanel became the epitome of bold and beautiful femininity, a symbol, and timeless icon.

But Coco did not just dress women – she truly empowered them through her fashion and her approach to life. With her statement pieces – a pantsuit for women (today popularly referred as the "power suit") that Marlene Dietrich and Katherine Hepburn first wore so spectacularly; the little black dress that became the essential piece of any woman's wardrobe; the pink suit from the 1961 autumn/winter collection that Jackie Kennedy sent off to eternity; the iconic Chanel No 5 that captures the scent of the seductive force of female sensuality – and many other pieces that revolutionized the way women not only looked but carried themselves through life by their own choice. Coco Chanel shared the boldness, passion and audacity she unapologetically lived by with all womankind.

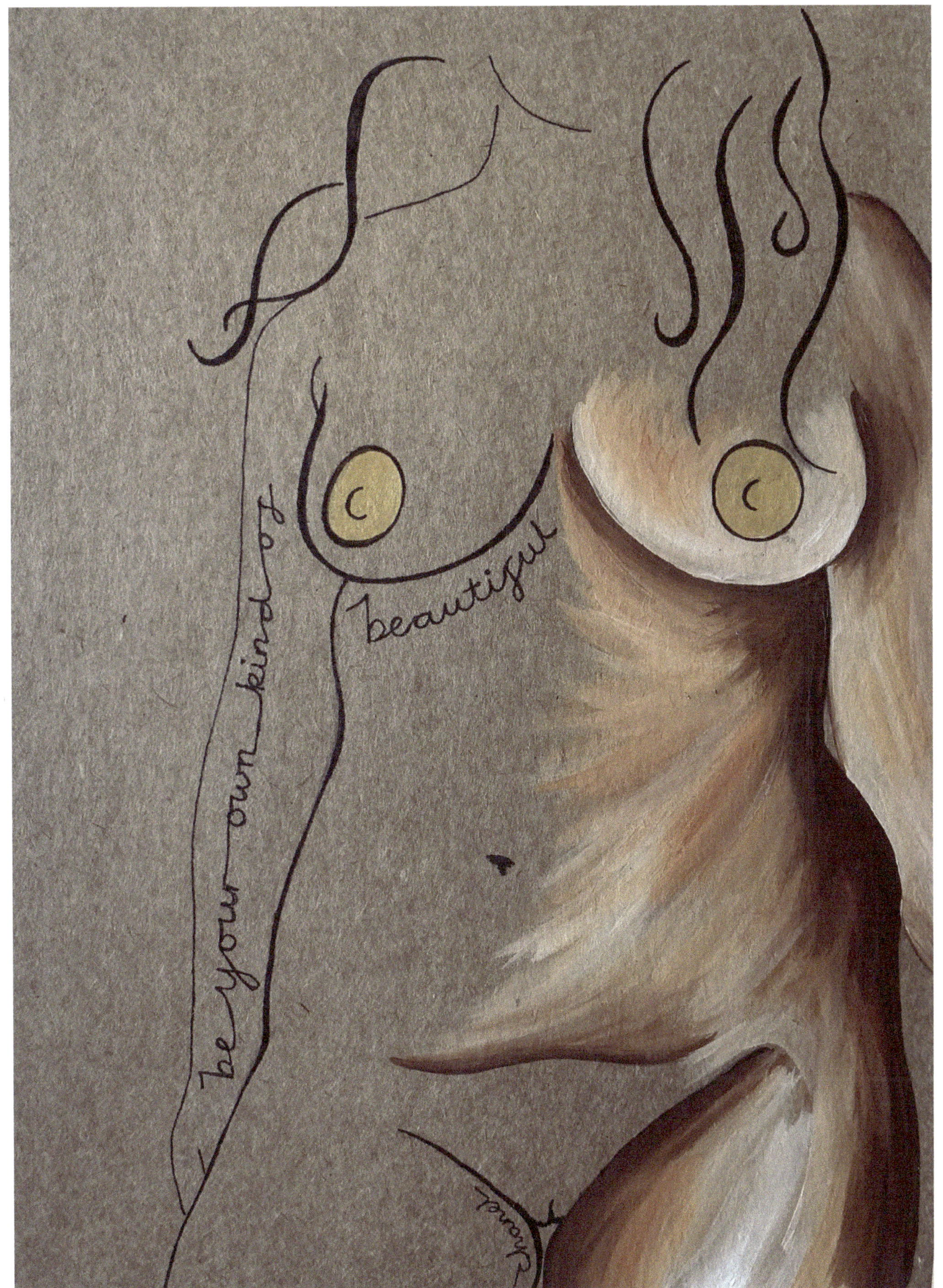
be your own kind of
beautiful

Audrey Hepburn (1929 – 1993) was a British actress and humanitarian. Recognised as both a film and fashion icon, she was ranked by the American Film Institute as the third-greatest female screen legend from the Golden Age of Hollywood and was inducted into the International Best Dressed List Hall of Fame. She was thought to have repeatedly struggled against the way women should dress, making trousers a female fashion statement – and often wore flats, giving women an out from towering stilettos.

Hepburn devoted the final years of her life to humanitarian work. Although she had contributed to them since 1954, Audrey Hepburn became a Goodwill Ambassador for UNICEF in 1988 – and she dedicated the rest of her life to helping impoverished children in Africa, Asia and Latin America by working in the field, nursing sick children and spreading awareness about conditions in these nations. In 1992 she received the Presidential Medal of Freedom. In addition to this award, she remains one of only 16 people who have won Academy, Emmy, Grammy, and Tony Awards.

Audrey Hepburn is a hero because she overcame adversity, helped others, and never gave up. She was in Holland when the Nazi's took over and watched German soldiers put men against a wall and shoot at them – her uncle being one of them. Her waif-like figure was the visual remnant of her starvation as a child during World War II, which resulted in a slew of ailments that led to "a lifetime of quietly suffering frail health." In short, her pain became her beauty – and by extension, her livelihood – and she then used her fame for good with UNICEF.

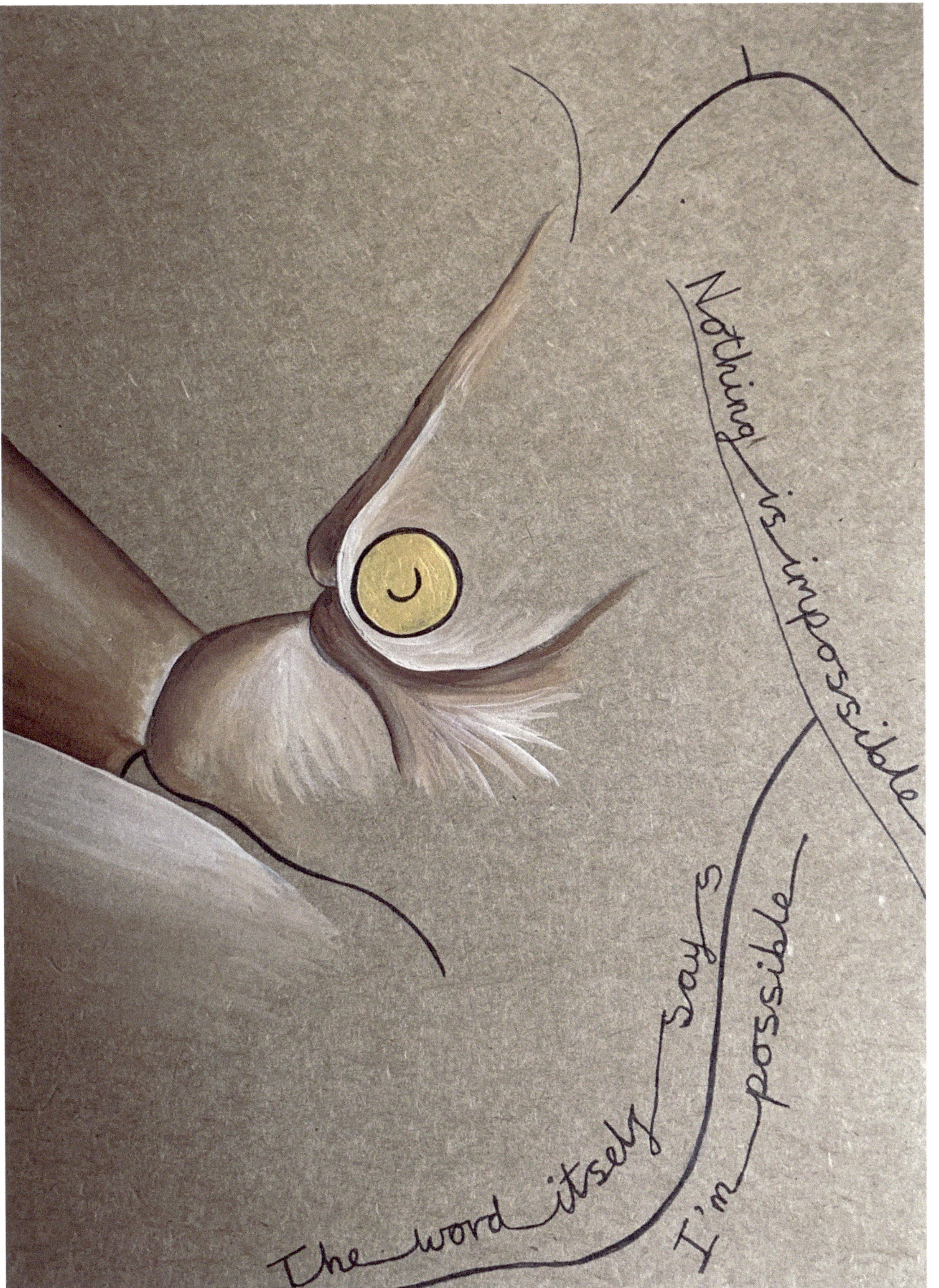

Nothing is impossible
The word itself says
I'm possible

Amelia Mary Earhart (1897 – 1937) was an American aviation pioneer and author. Earhart was the first female aviator to fly solo across the Atlantic Ocean. She set many other records and wrote best-selling books about her flying experiences. She was instrumental in the formation of The Ninety-Nines, an organization for female pilots where she was elected president – which still exists today. It was on June 18th 1928 when Amelia Earhart succeeded in her dream of being the first female pilot to fly across the Atlantic Ocean (3875 km) solo – even though the dangerous journey had only ever been completed solo once before by a man and many others had died attempting it. It wasn't an easy journey, with her entering a storm near Paris – where she was initially supposed to land. This caused mechanical issues and she thought fast, changing course to land safely in Londonderry, Northern Ireland after a 14-hour and 56-minute flight. She was the 16th woman to be issued a pilot's license.

Her impressive achievements garnered her much support in the public eye, and her various successes as a female pilot even inspired future generations of young women to pursue careers in aviation.

Earhart solidified her legacy as a force by publishing a book about her trans-Atlantic flight, touring the nation giving lectures on her success, and becoming an editor at *Cosmopolitan* magazine as well as serving as an official for the National Aeronautic Association.

Sadly, Amelia Earhart mysteriously disappeared during a flight in 1937 over the Pacific Ocean whilst trying to be the first woman to fly the entire world. Despite a huge rescue attempt, she was never found and was pronounced legally dead 2 years later. Although she is perhaps most well-known as the pilot who disappeared mysteriously while flying over the Pacific Ocean, we must not eclipse Earhart's legacy as one of the most successful female aviators in history. We must reclaim her truth as a trailblazing aviatrix, inspiring generations of women to pursue traditionally male-dominated careers with the same grit and determination that she had. Earhart always worked to portray her individual achievements as examples of what women could do if given a chance.

Earhart's accomplishments were liberating for females all around the world. After completing various record-breaking flights, she received hundreds of letters and telegrams congratulating her success. The majority, if not most, of Earhart's career was defined by pushing society's rigid boundaries and making a place for herself in a man's world without asking permission.

The woman who can create her own job is the one who will win fame & fortune
Amelia Earhart

"There is no limit to what we, as women, can accomplish."

Michelle LaVaughn Robinson Obama (born 17th January 1964) is an American attorney and author who was the First Lady of the United States from 2009 to 2017. She is married to the 44th president of the United States, Barack Obama, and was the first African American First Lady.

Michelle has been creating her own legacy in many ways, including the "Let Girls Learn" initiative started in March 2015. The idea behind this program is to help educate the 62 million girls around the world who aren't in school. She says: "I see myself in these girls, I see my daughters in these girls, and I simply cannot walk away from them. I plan to keep raising my voice on their behalf for the rest of my life. I plan to keep urging world leaders to invest in their potential and create societies that truly value them as human beings. I plan to keep reaching out to local leaders, families, and girls themselves to raise awareness about the power of sending girls to school."

Her speeches are always full of inspiration. One of her most famous speeches consisted of the following inspirational words: "The women we honour today teach us three very important lessons. One, that as women, we must stand up for ourselves. The second, as women, we must stand up for each other. And finally, as women, we must stand up for justice for all."

She also spoke directly to men at the United State of Women Summit. "Be better at everything. Be better fathers. Good lord, just being good fathers who love your daughters and are providing a solid example of what it means to be a good man in the world, showing them what it feels like to be loved. That is the greatest gift that the men in my life gave to me."

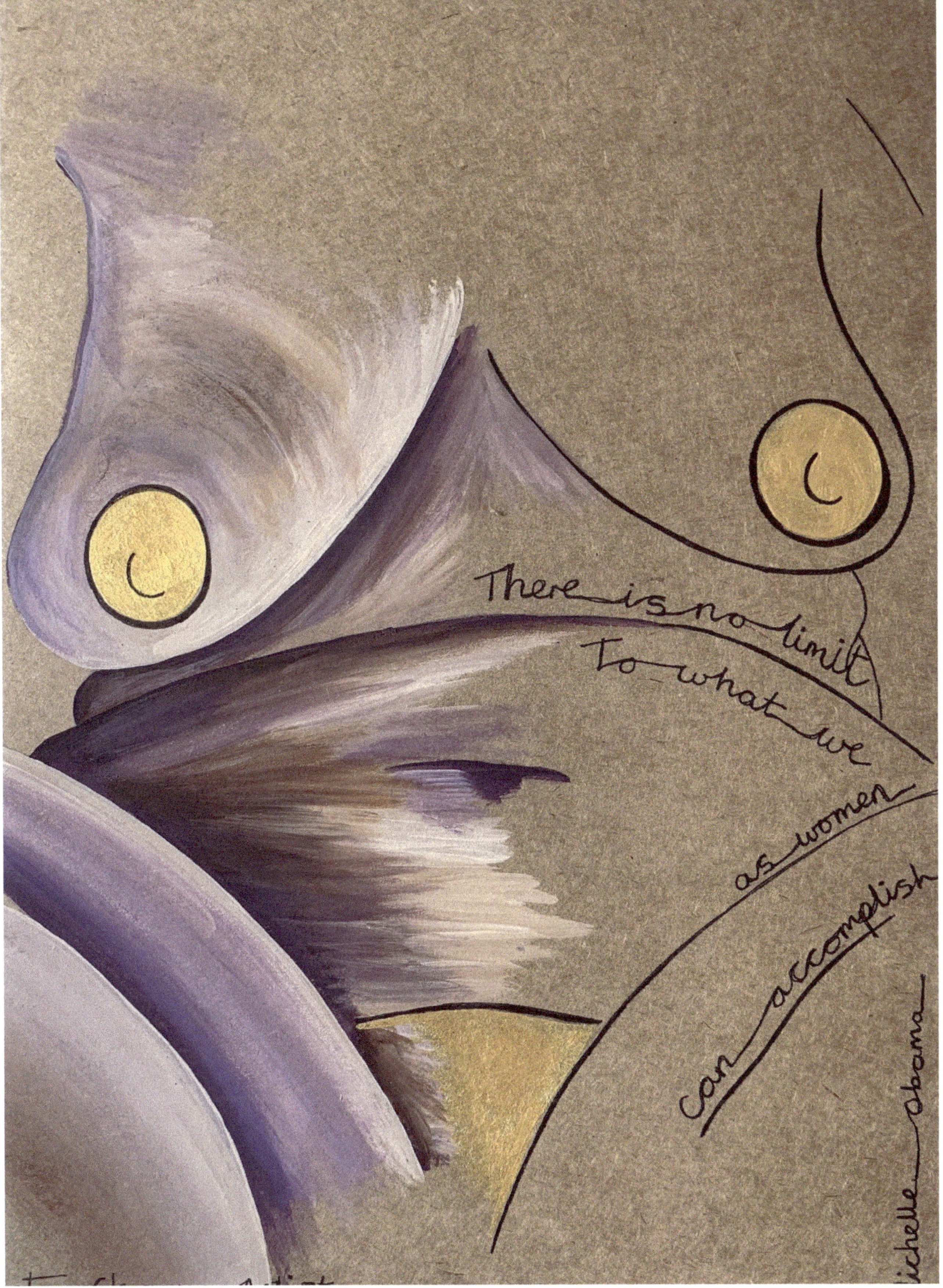

There is no limit
To what we
as women
can accomplish
Michelle Obama

"I'll be fierce for all of us."

Debra Anne Haaland (born in December, 1960) is an American politician who has been the U.S. Representative from New Mexico's 1st congressional district since 2019. She is the first Native American cabinet secretary, as an enrolled member of the Laguna Pueblo, one of 574 sovereign tribal nations located across 35 states. The Pueblo people have lived on the land that is now the state of New Mexico since the 1200s and Haaland identifies herself as a 35th-generation New Mexican.

Debra Haaland is making American HERstory. In her position, she has responsibility for the country's land and natural resources as head of the Department of the Interior – as well as upholding the government's legally binding obligations to the tribes.

In an interview days before her nomination, Haaland said that as secretary of the interior she would "move climate change priorities, tribal consultation and a green economic recovery forward." And in her acceptance speech she said, "I'll be fierce for all of us, for our planet, and all of our protected land."

Representation and diversity matter, according to Haaland, because life experiences shape political decisions. "We don't need people who all have the same perspective, we need people from various parts of the country, who've been raised in different ways, who bring that history and culture with them, and employ what we've learnt from their parents and grandparents, and bring all of that to bear in the decisions that we make."

It's been a rocky road for Haaland who has experienced homelessness and relied on food stamps. She is also the product of racist policies. "There are a lot of people in this country who suffered historical trauma. I carry history with me, I'm a product of the assimilation policy of the United States. I feel very strongly that having this perspective is super important for the issues we bring to Congress."

Haaland was elected to the House of Representatives in 2018 after campaigning under the slogan, "Congress has never heard a voice like mine." Since then, she has introduced legislation that would establish a truth commission on Native American boarding schools and spearheaded two laws to combat the epidemic of missing and murdered indigenous women.

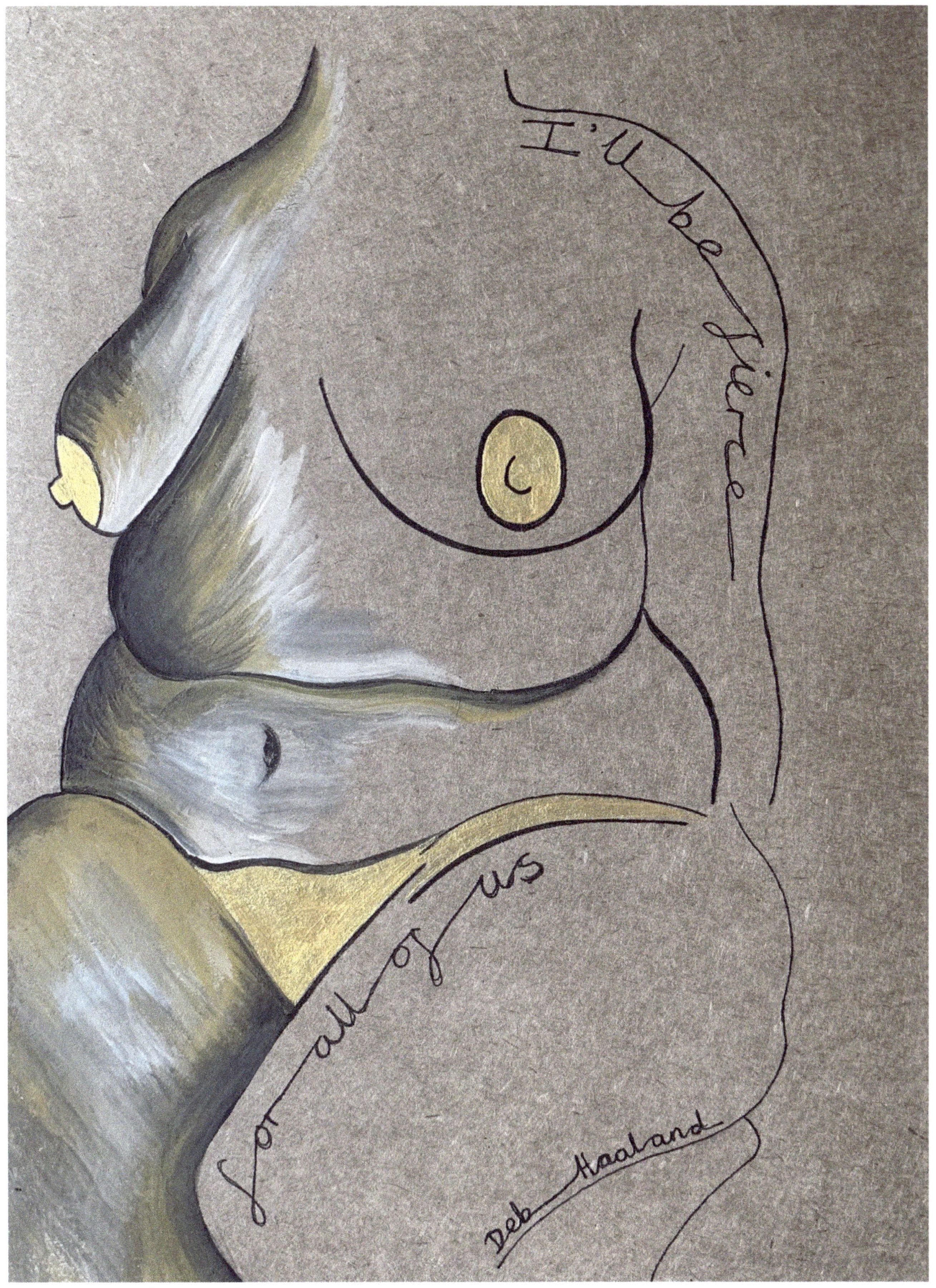

I'll be fierce
for all of us
Deb Haaland

**"The emotional, sexual and psychological stereotyping of females begins
when the doctor says: 'it's a girl."**

Shirley Anita Chisholm (1924 – 2005) was an American politician, educator, and author. In 1968,
she made HERstory by becoming the first Black woman elected to the United States Congress,
representing New York's 12th congressional district for seven terms from 1969 to 1983. The Brooklyn-
born activist and political leader later entered the 1975 democratic presidential race – the first woman
and the first Black American to do this.

In Congress she quickly became known as a strong liberal who opposed weapons development and the
war in Vietnam. Chisholm, a founder of the National Women's Political Caucus, supported the Equal
Rights Amendment and legalized abortions throughout her congressional career, which lasted from
1969 to 1983. She later wrote the autobiographical works *Unbought and Unbossed* (1970) and *The
Good Fight* (1973).

Shirley Chisholm's signature campaign slogan, "Unbought and unbossed," was as much a statement
about who she was as it was a catchy and effective message that helped her become the first Black
woman elected to Congress. She described herself as "the people's politician," fighting for higher wages
for working people and more money for public education and demanding respect for Black Americans
and women. When she got to Capitol Hill, she challenged institutional customs, pushing her way into
spaces that had been the reserve of white men and making friends and enemies on both sides of the
aisle by following her own political playbook.

Chisholm's persona – an independent, outspoken, advocate for marginalized groups and liberal causes
– often put her at odds with the establishment. She both embraced and pushed back against efforts to
label her. In her speech announcing her presidential campaign she declared: "I am not the candidate
of Black America, although I am Black and proud. I am not the candidate of the women's movement of
this country, although I am a woman, and I am equally proud of that. I am the candidate of the people
of America."

Her forceful confrontation of those who would try to constrain her because of her race and gender is
what has made her political identity a template for a new generation.

Shirley Chisholm died on Jan. 1, 2005, at the age of 80, leaving her giant mark on the world and
changing HERstory forever.

The emotional sexual and psychological stereotyping of females

begins when the doctor says "it's a girl"

Shirley Chisholm

"We realise the importance of our own voices only when we are silenced."

Malala Yousafzai was born on 12th July 1997, and is often referred to just as Malala. She is a
Pakistani activist for female education and the youngest Nobel Prize winner after surviving a gunshot
wound to the face by the Taliban. She has since become a spokesperson for human rights,
education and women's rights. In many parts of the world, girls are subjected to brutal violence
and cannot live freely, with over 130 million of them not allowed an education. Malala fights for their
rights, and although the Taliban tried to silence her by killing her, they gave her an even stronger voice,
which is heard all over the world.

When Malala was born, her arrival wasn't celebrated as much as it would've been if she'd been a boy.
Most Pashtun people (from the Swat Valley) believed that boys were more important than girls. But
Malala's father Ziauddin was different and from the beginning he encouraged her to be all she could
be. She spent a lot of time at her father's school in the city learning not only academic lessons but also
how different boys' and girls' lives were, and how men are were always in charge. But she also learnt
from her father that things didn't have to be like that, as he fought for everyone's right to go to school.
When Malala was ten years old, the Taliban came to the Swat Valley. They gathered people's CDs, DVDs
and televisions, and burnt them in huge piles on the street, soon setting their sights on girls' schools,
and by 2008 the Taliban began blowing them up. When Malala was eleven, she was interviewed on
several TV channels, speaking out for girls' right to go to school and in a BBC interview in Urdu, she
said: "How dare the Taliban take away my right to education?" It was soon announced that all schools
for girls were closing. Malala started to write a diary and excerpts were read out on BBC radio, talking
about how it felt to be afraid, about the ban on girls going to school, and about being forced to wear a
burka and hide her face.

Widespread protests caused the Taliban to allow girls up to the age of ten to attend school, but Malala
and her friends were too old, so they continued to study in secret, hiding their school books under
their shawls. Malala said, "We want to be able to make our own decisions – nowhere in the Koran does
it say that a woman should be dependent on a man or have to listen to one."

The Taliban soon issued death threats against her, and one day, two men dressed in white stepped out
onto the road, forcing her school bus to make an emergency stop. Climbing into the back, one of them
shouted "Which one of you is Malala?" She was the only one without her face covered, and the man
lifted his gun firing three rapid shots. The first hit Malala in the head and she was flown to hospital, not
regaining consciousness for a week and waking with one half of her face paralysed. Yet she recovered
and on 12 July 2013, the day that Malala turned 16, she was invited to the United Nations, where she
said "Today is the day of every woman, boy and girl who has raised their voice for their rights. Let us
wage a global struggle against illiteracy, poverty and terrorism. Let us pick up our books and pens, they
are our most powerful weapons. Education first – extremists have shown what frightens them most – a
girl with a book. With guns you can kill terrorists, but with education you can kill terrorism."

We realise the importance of our own voices
only when we are
Silenced
Malala Yousafzai

"Every individual matters.
Every individual has a role to play.
Every individual makes a difference."

Dame Jane Morris Goodall DBE (born on 3rd April 1934), is an English primatologist and anthropologist. In July 1960, at the age of 26, she travelled from England to what is now Tanzania and ventured into the little-known world of wild chimpanzees. She began studying them in the Gombe Stream National Park of Tanzania, and her extensive research (which spanned almost 60 years) has provided some of the most ground-breaking insight into the minds and social lives of chimpanzees.

When Jane Goodall entered the forest of Gombe, the world knew very little about chimpanzees, and even less about their unique genetic kinship to humans. She took an unorthodox approach in her field research, immersing herself in their habitat and their lives to experience their complex society as a neighbour rather than a distant observer. She came to understand them not only as a species, but also as individuals with emotions and long-term bonds. Dr. Jane Goodall's discovery in 1960 that chimpanzees make and use tools is considered one of the greatest achievements of twentieth-century scholarship. Her field research at Gombe transformed our understanding of chimpanzees and redefined the relationship between humans and animals in ways that continue to emanate around the world.

The primatologist and anthropologist went on to found the Jane Goodall Institute in 1977 as well as the Roots and Shoots program in 1991 in an effort to encourage wildlife conservation. She is desperate to bring to our attention the urgent need to protect chimpanzees from extinction and travels the world, speaking about the threats facing chimpanzees and environmental crises, urging each of us to take action on behalf of all living things and the planet we share.

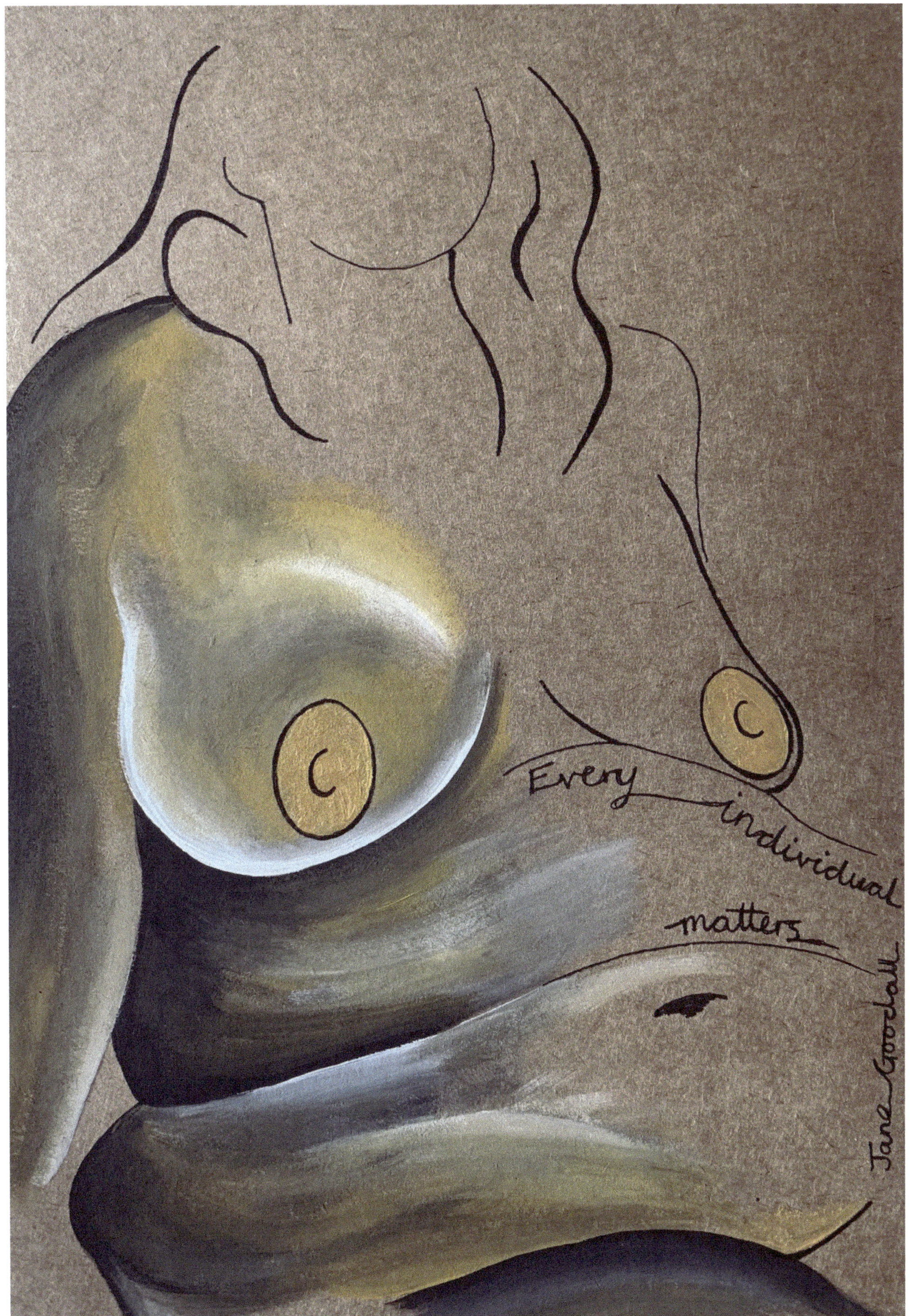

Every individual matters
Jane Goodall

"You alone are enough."

Maya Angelou (1928 – 2014) was an amazing woman with an incredible life story, and her name is known by almost everybody who hears it. She was an American poet, memoirist, and civil rights activist who published seven autobiographies, three books of essays, several books of poetry – and is also credited with a list of plays, movies, and television shows spanning over 50 years. In her life, Maya Angelou received dozens of awards and more than 50 honorary degrees.

When she was 8 years old, Maya Angelou totally stopped speaking. She silenced her voice because she thought that in her using her voice, she had killed a man. For almost five years, she spoke to no one but her beloved brother, Bailey. But when her voice did come back, she most definitely used it to maximise the impact that she made on the world.

I Know Why the Caged Bird Sings, Angelou's groundbreaking memoir (and first book) about her childhood, was published in 1969 – when she was 41 years old. She spoke her truth and her voice was established again – the one she had silenced as a child. But this time, her voice was louder than ever and became one of the most important voices in American literature.

Her work and her life offer readers a personal journey through the African American experience of the 20th century, writing with blazing honesty about racism, her pregnancy at 16 and the deep fractures in her own family. Her strong voice speaks to countless readers as her themes of finding identity, strength, economic, racial, and sexual oppression and courage carry deep resonance. Besides writing of racial inequality, Angelou wrote many empowering poems about women and their rights; she wrote about the hypocrisy of the world, and injustice, but also about love and nature.

One of Angelou's most recognizable poems is one about the power of women titled "Phenomenal Woman." In this poem, Angelou speaks out about the dignity of being a woman, about self-pride and female grace. It is about sex appeal and the inner power that radiates through in an inexplicable way. This kind of strength has nothing to do with a dress size or other beauty standards that are imposed on women:; it has a deeper meaning, as it is connected to each woman's divine feminine identity. And another – "Still I Rise," talks of the unstoppable determination and grit of woman to rise from every situation or type of oppression.

An amazing woman who has shaped HERstory.

You
Alone
Are enough
Maya Angelou

"You are powerful and your voice matters."

Kamala Devi Harris (born on 20th October 1964) is an American politician and attorney who is the 49th and current Vice President of the United States. She is the United States' first female Vice President, the highest-ranking female elected official in U.S. history, and the first African American and first Asian American vice president.

Harris was born in Oakland, California, in 1964, to parents who raised her in a bassinet of civil rights activism. Her mother, Shyamala Gopalan Harris, an Indian immigrant, was a breast cancer researcher who died of cancer in 2009. Harris' father, Donald, is a Jamaican American professor of economics. On the campaign trail, the vice president-elect often talked about how her activist parents would push her in her stroller at civil rights marches.

Kamala Harris is a lot of things beyond her gender and her race of course. But her mere presence brings so much with it to so many women and girls of all ages across the whole world, showing them that stereotypes can be broken and big achievements can be made by anyone – including all who see themselves within Kamala Harris in some way.

"Because every little girl watching tonight sees that this is a country of possibilities, and to the children of our country, regardless of your gender, our country has sent you a clear message: Dream with ambition, lead with conviction and see yourselves in a way that others may not, simply because they've never seen it before. But know that we will applaud you every step of the way."

For countless women and girls, Harris' achievement of reaching the second highest office in America represents hope, validation and the shattering of the proverbial glass ceiling that has kept mostly white men perched at the tiers of the American government. But these ripples of hope and change ripple out to every corner of the world as Kamala Harris proves that women can step into uncharted territories never before dwelled by women, and take their place with confidence.

No wonder she has become so inspiring!

you are powerful
and your voice matters
Kamala Harris

"Aging is not lost youth but a new stage of opportunity and strength."

Betty Friedan (1921 – 2006) was an American feminist writer, journalist, activist, and co-founder of the National Organization for Women. Betty Friedan was one of the early leaders of the women's rights movement of the 1960s and 1970s. Her 1963 best-selling book, _The Feminine Mystique_, gave voice to millions of American women's frustrations with their limited gender roles and helped spark widespread public activism for gender equality.

Published in 1963, _The Feminine Mystique_ hit a nerve, becoming an instant best-seller that continues to be regarded as one of the most influential nonfiction books of the 20th century. Women everywhere voiced a similar "malaise" from what Friedan dubbed, "the problem that has no name." The book helped transform public awareness and brought many women into the vanguard of the women's movement, just as it propelled Friedan into its early leadership.

In 1966, Friedan joined forces with Pauli Murray and Aileen Hernandez to found the National Organization for Women, with Friedan as its first president. She also authored NOW's mission statement: "...to bring women into full participation in the mainstream of American society now, exercising all the privileges and responsibilities thereof in truly equal partnership with men." The organization's first action: to demand Equal Employment Opportunities!

Friedan helped found the National Association for the Repeal of Abortion Laws in 1969, later renamed National Abortion Rights Action League and more recently NARAL Pro-choice America. She organized the Women's Strike for Equality on August 26, 1970 on the 50th anniversary of Women's Suffrage, to raise awareness about gender discrimination. In addition, in 1971, Friedan was a co-founder of the National Women's Political Caucus with Congresswoman Bella Abzug, Congresswoman Shirley Chisholm, and feminist Gloria Steinem. Through these organizations, Friedan was influential in changing outdated laws such as unfair hiring practices, gender pay inequality and pregnancy discrimination.

Regardless of the country you live in, the sheer determination of Berry Friedan to "bring women into truly equal partnerships with men" definitely established her as a woman who has shaped HERStory for future generations to come.

Aging is not lost youth but a new stage of opportunity and strength
Betty Friedan

"I can excuse anything except boredom."

Hedy Lamarr (1914 – 2000) was an Austrian-American actress and inventor who pioneered the technology that would one day form the basis for today's WiFi, GPS, and Bluetooth communication systems. A natural beauty, she was seen widely on the big screen in films like *Samson and Delilah* and *White Cargo.*

Lamarr was originally Hedwig Eva Kiesler, born in Vienna, Austria on November 9th, 1914 into a well-to-do Jewish family. An only child, Lamarr received a great deal of attention from her father, a bank director and curious man, who inspired her to look at the world with open eyes. He would often take her for long walks where he would discuss the inner workings of different machines, like the printing press or street cars. These conversations guided Lamarr's thinking and at only 5 years of age, she could be found taking apart and reassembling her music box to understand how the machine operated. Meanwhile, Lamarr's mother was a concert pianist and introduced her to the arts, placing her in both ballet and piano lessons at a young age.

Lamarr's brilliant mind was ignored, and her beauty took centre stage when she was discovered by director Max Reinhardt at age 16. She studied acting with Reinhardt in Berlin and was in her first small film role by 1930. It wasn't until 1932 that Lamarr gained name recognition as an actress for her role in the controversial film, *Ecstasy.*

Lamarr was indeed a genius as the gears in her inventive mind continued to turn. She once said, "Improving things comes naturally to me." Her most significant invention was engineered as the United States geared up to enter World War II.

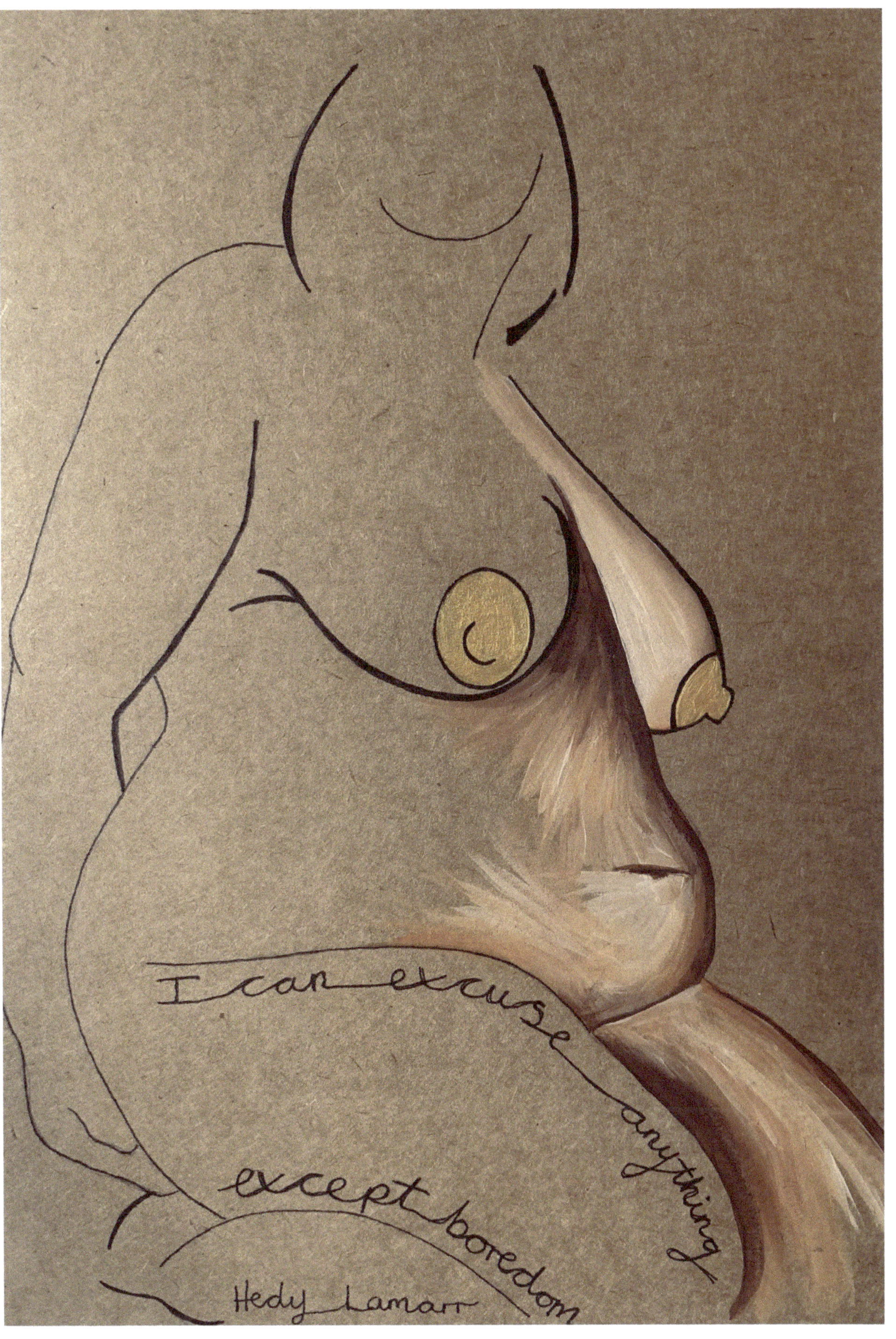

I can excuse anything
except boredom
Hedy Lamarr

"I am my own muse."

Magdalena Carmen Frida Kahlo y Calderón (1907 – 1954) was a Mexican painter known for her many portraits, self-portraits, and works inspired by the nature and artifacts of Mexico. A force in the art world, Frida Kahlo was known around the world for creating thought-provoking works grounded in magical realism. Her 1938 self-portrait titled "the frame" was the first work by a 20th century Mexican artist to ever be featured in the Louvre.

Her pain, passion, and bold, vibrant colours are recognized in every piece of her artwork and she is celebrated in Mexico for her attention to Mexican and indigenous culture and by feminists for her depiction of the female experience and form.

Kahlo, who suffered from polio as a child, nearly died in a bus accident as a teenager. She suffered multiple fractures of her spine, collarbone and ribs, a shattered pelvis, broken foot and a dislocated shoulder. She began to focus heavily on painting while recovering in a body cast. In her lifetime, she had 30 operations.

Life experience is a common theme in Kahlo's approximately 200 paintings, sketches and drawings. Her physical and emotional pain are depicted starkly on canvases, as is her turbulent relationship with her husband, fellow artist Diego Rivera, who she married twice. Of her 143 paintings, 55 are self-portraits. During her life, self-portraits are a subject that Frida Kahlo always returns to, she says: "I paint self-portraits because I am so often alone, because I am the person I know best."

Spirited, unyielding and bold, Frida Kahlo was a woman who dared to defy the circumstances of her unfortunate life. Her works of art may have showcased great talent, but it was her tenacity in the face of hardship and a gender-biased society that have become valuable inspiration for many.

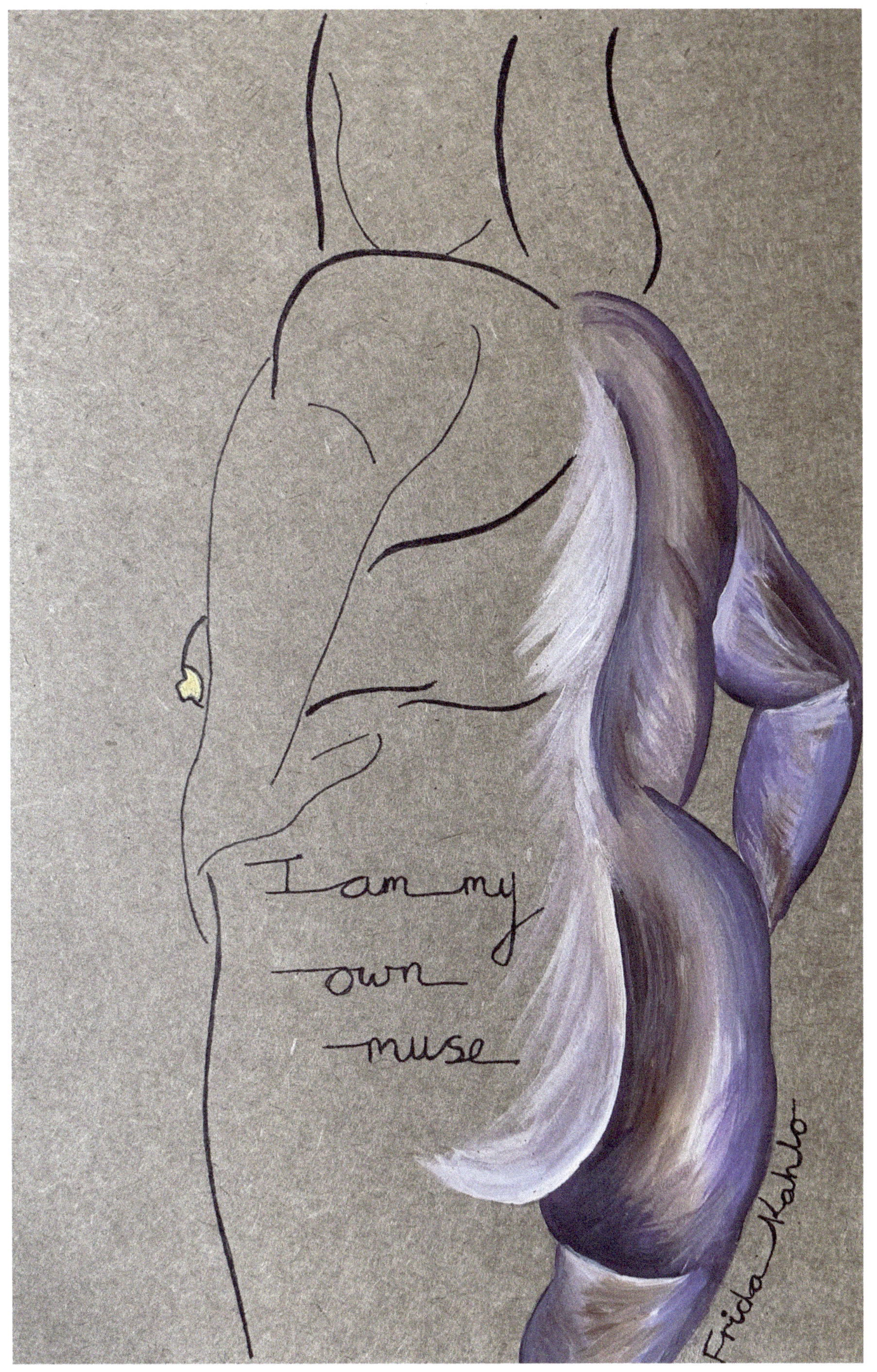

I am my
own
muse
Frida Kahlo

"The most dangerous phrase in the language is: it's always been that way."

At a very young age **Grace Murray Hopper** (1906 – 1992) showed an interest in engineering. As a child, she would often take apart household goods and put them back together. Little did her family know that her curiosity would eventually gain her recognition from the highest office in the land.

Hopper earned her Masters and PhD in Mathematics from Yale – becoming one of the very few women to hold such a credential. She joined the Navy WAVES (Women Accepted for Voluntary Emergency Service) and in 1944, was commissioned as a Lieutenant (Junior Grade) and assigned to the Bureau of Ordnance Computation Project at Harvard University. Her team worked on and produced the Mark I, an early prototype of the electronic computer and coined the word "bug" to describe a computer malfunction.

After the end of the war, Hopper became a research fellow on the Harvard faculty. In 1949, she joined the Eckert-Mauchly Corporation, continuing her pioneering work on computer technology. Hopper was involved in the creation of UNIVAC, the first all-electronic digital computer. She invented the first computer compiler, a program that translates written instructions into codes that computers read directly. This work led her to co-develop COBOL, one of the earliest standardized computer languages. COBOL enabled computers to respond to words in addition to numbers. Hopper also lectured widely on computers, delivering up to 300 lectures per year. She predicted that computers would one day be small enough to fit on a desk and people who were not professional programmers would use them in their everyday life.

In 1973, Hopper was named a distinguished fellow of the British Computer Society – the first and only woman to hold the title at that time.

The most dangerous
phrase in the language
is: It's always
been that
way

Grace Hopper

"You must do the thing you think you cannot do."

A shy, insecure child, **Eleanor Roosevelt** (1884 – 1962) would grow up to become one of the most important and beloved First Ladies, authors, reformers, and female leaders of the 20th century. Born on October 11, 1884 in New York City, Anna Eleanor Roosevelt was the first of Elliot and Anna Hall Roosevelt's three children. Her family was affluent and politically prominent, and while her childhood was in many ways blessed, it was also marked by hardship: her father's alcoholism, as well as the deaths of both parents and one of her brothers before she was ten years old. She was raised by her harsh and critical maternal grandmother, who damaged Eleanor's self-esteem. Timid and awkward, she believed that she compared badly with other girls.

In the White House from 1933 to 1945, First Lady Roosevelt kept a dizzying schedule. She wrote nearly 3,000 articles in newspapers and magazines, including a monthly column in *Women's Home Companion*, donating what she earned from the column to charity. She also authored six books and travelled nationwide delivering countless speeches. She held weekly press conferences with women reporters who she hoped would get her message to the American people.

Roosevelt had immense influence on her husband's decisions as president and in shaping America, and her political activism did not end with her husband's death in 1945. Appointed in 1946, she served for more than a decade as a delegate to the United Nations, the institution established by her husband, and embraced the cause of world peace.

She dramatically changed the role of the first lady, advocating for human rights, women's rights and children's causes, and has definitely made history HERstory.

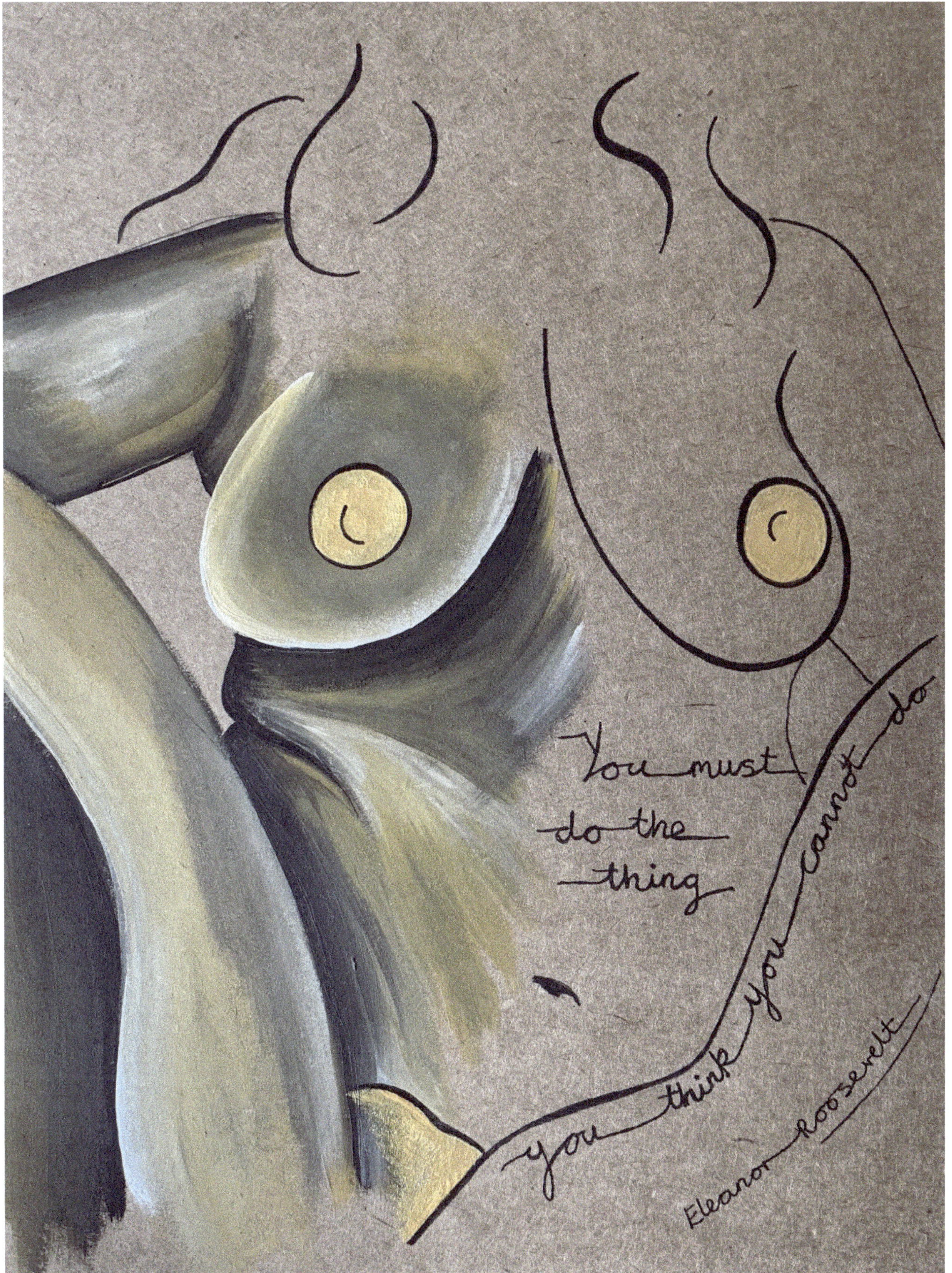

You must
do the
thing
you think you cannot do
Eleanor Roosevelt

"Have no fear of perfection, you will never reach it."

Marie Skłodowska Curie (1867 – 1934), born Maria Salomea Skłodowska, was a Polish and naturalized-French physicist and chemist who conducted pioneering research on radioactivity. Born in Warsaw on November 7, 1867, the daughter of a secondary-school teacher, she received a general education in local schools and some scientific training from her father. She became involved in a students' revolutionary organization and in 1891, she went to Paris to continue her studies at the Sorbonne where she obtained awards in Physics and the Mathematical Sciences. She met Pierre Curie, Professor in the School of Physics in 1894 and in the following year they were married. She succeeded her husband as Head of the Physics Laboratory at the Sorbonne, gained her Doctor of Science degree in 1903, and following the tragic death of Pierre in 1906, she took his place as Professor of General Physics in the Faculty of Sciences, the first time a woman had held this position. She was also appointed Director of the Curie Laboratory in the Radium Institute of the University of Paris, founded in 1914.

Her early research with her husband was often performed under difficult conditions. Laboratory arrangements were poor and both had to undertake much teaching to earn a livelihood. The Curies were inspired by Henri Becquerel's discovery of radioactivity in 1896 – which led them to the isolation of polonium (named after the country of Marie's birth) and later, to the discovery of radium. Marie Curie developed methods for the separation of radium from radioactive residues in sufficient quantities to allow for its characterization and the careful study of its properties, therapeutic properties in particular, and was held in high esteem and admiration by scientists throughout the world.

The importance of Marie Curie's work is reflected in the numerous awards bestowed on her. She received many honorary science, medicine and law degrees and honorary memberships of learned societies throughout the world. Together with her husband, she was awarded half of the Nobel Prize for Physics in 1903, and in 1911 she received a second Nobel Prize – this time in Chemistry, in recognition of her work in radioactivity. She also received, jointly with her husband, the Davy Medal of the Royal Society in 1903. In 1921, President Harding of the United States, on behalf of the women of America, presented her with one gram of radium in recognition of her service to science. Marie Curie is remembered for her huge contribution to finding treatments for cancer.

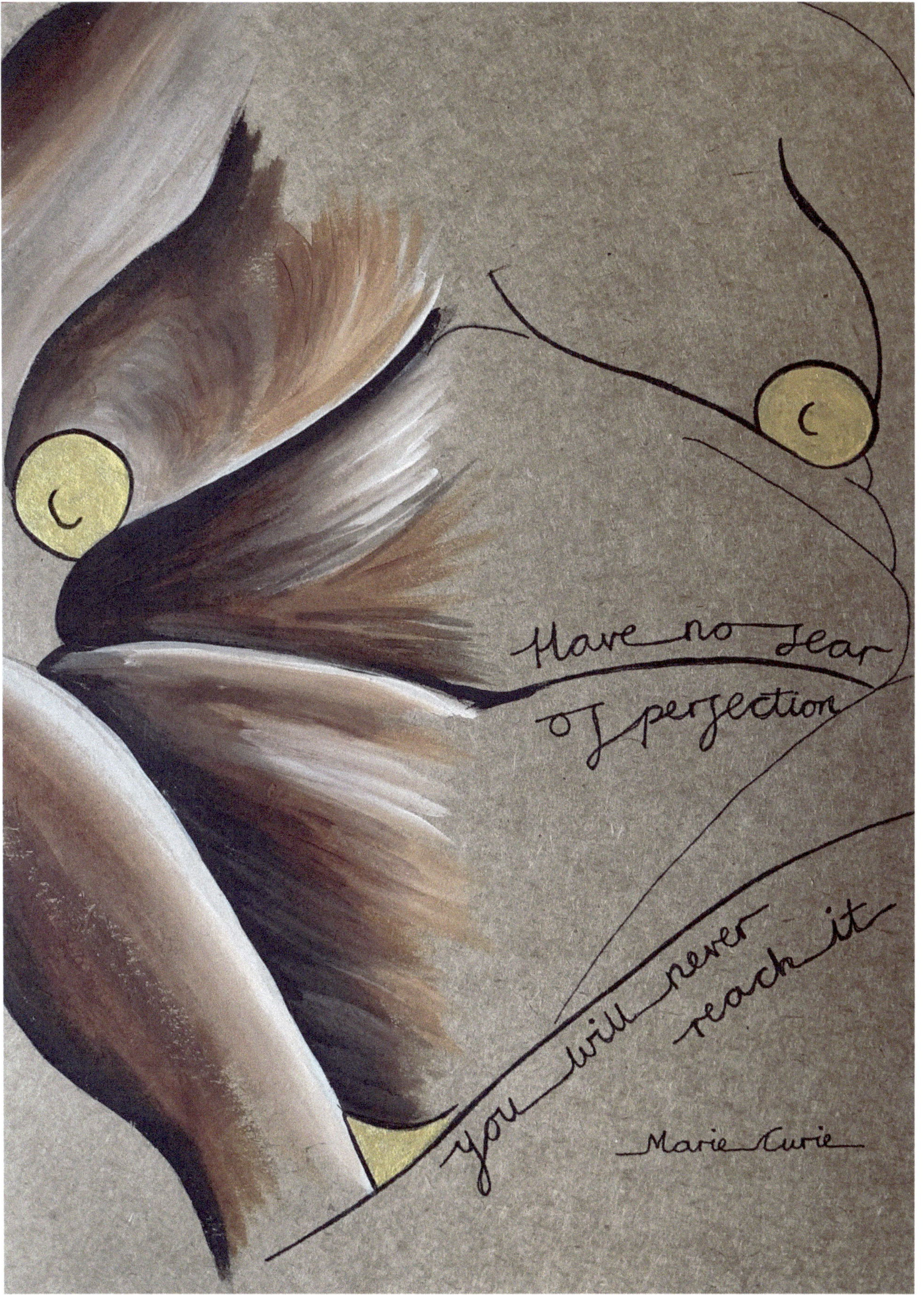
Have no fear
of perfection
you will never
reach it
Marie Curie

"Spread love everywhere you go."

Mother Mary Teresa Bojaxhiu (1910 – 1997), honoured in the Catholic Church as Saint Teresa of Calcutta, was an Albanian-Indian Roman Catholic nun and missionary. At the age of twelve, she strongly felt the call of God, and knew she had to be a missionary to spread the love. At the age of eighteen she left her parental home in Skopje and joined the Sisters of Loreto, an Irish community of nuns with missions in India. After a few months of training in Dublin she was sent to India, where on May 24, 1931, she took her initial vows as a nun.

From 1931 to 1948 Mother Teresa taught at St. Mary's High School in Calcutta, but the suffering and poverty she glimpsed outside the convent walls made such a deep impression on her that in 1948 she received permission from her superiors to leave the convent school and devote herself to working among the poorest of the poor in the slums of Calcutta. Although she had no funds, she depended on Divine Providence, and started an open-air school for slum children. Soon she was joined by voluntary helpers, and financial support was also forthcoming. This made it possible for her to extend the scope of her work.

On October 7, 1950, Mother Teresa received permission from the Holy See to start her own order, "The Missionaries of Charity," whose primary task was to love and care for those persons nobody was prepared to look after. In 1965, the Society became an International Religious Family by a decree of Pope Paul VI.

The Society of Missionaries has spread all over the world, providing effective help to the poorest of the poor in many countries in Asia, Africa, and Latin America. They undertake relief work in the wake of natural catastrophes such as floods, epidemics, and famine, and for refugees. The order also has houses in North America, Europe and Australia, where they take care of shut-ins, alcoholics, homeless, and AIDS sufferers.

Mother Teresa's work has been recognised and acclaimed throughout the world and she has received a number of awards and distinctions, including the Pope John XXIII Peace Prize (1971) and the Nehru Prize for her promotion of international peace and understanding (1972). She also received the Balzan Prize (1979) and the Templeton and Magsaysay awards.

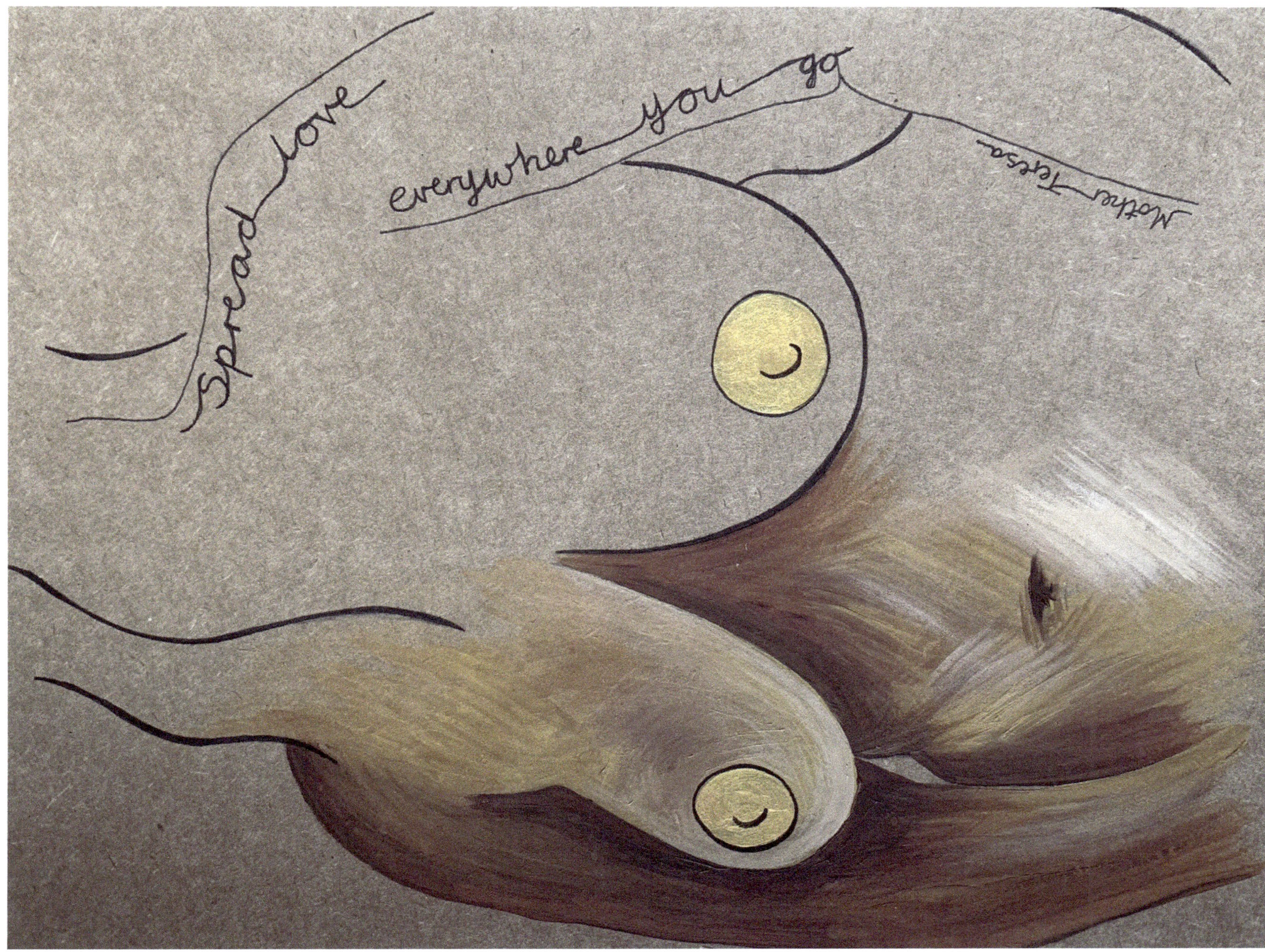

Spread love
everywhere you go
Mother Teresa

**"To all the girls who think you're fat because you're not a size zero,
you're the beautiful one, it's society who is ugly."**

Marilyn Monroe (1926 – 1962) was an American actress, model, and singer. Famous for playing comedic "blonde bombshell" characters, she became one of the most popular sex symbols of the 1950s and early 1960s and was emblematic of the era's changing attitudes toward sexuality.

Born Norma Jeane Mortenson in Los Angeles, California, she was later given her mother's name, and baptized Norma Jeane Baker. After a tumultuous childhood – both maternal grandparents and her mother were committed to mental institutions and she lived with a string of foster families – Norma Jeane married one of her neighbours, James Dougherty, when she was 16. He later joined the Merchant Marines and was sent to the South Pacific during World War II. A photographer "discovered" the naturally photogenic Norma Jeane while she was working in a California ammunition factory, and she was soon launched into a successful modelling career. She divorced Dougherty in June 1946 and soon after signed a film contract with 20th Century Fox.

At the outset of her acting career, Norma Jeane dyed her brown hair blonde and changed her name again, calling herself Marilyn Monroe, going on to star in films such as *Gentleman Prefer Blondes*, *How to Marry a Millionaire* and *Some like it Hot*. In January 1954, she married baseball star Joe DiMaggio but he was notoriously uncomfortable with his wife's sexy public image, and her wild popularity. They divorced after only nine months of marriage but remained good friends.

By 1961, trouble in Monroe's personal life – her third marriage to the acclaimed playwright Arthur Miller, dissolved after four years – led to her increasing emotional fragility, and that year she was admitted on two occasions to hospitals for psychiatric observation. On August 5, 1962, Marilyn Monroe was found dead from an overdose of barbiturates in her home in Brentwood, California. She was 36 years old.

Since she was such a complex character, Marilyn Monroe found herself stuck in the middle of two different types of women: those who were disgusted or intimidated by her glamour and wanted her to tone everything down, and those who loved her look just as it was and wanted her to stop trying to be taken seriously. Marilyn shared her views on the subject in 1959: "I'd like to be known as a real actress and human being," she said, "but listen, there's nothing wrong with glamour either. I think everything adds up. I'll never knock glamour. But I want to be in the kind of pictures where I can develop seriously as a woman, not just wear tights."

Marilyn was a strong woman who consistently fought for what she believed in.

To all the girls
who think you're fat
because you're
not a size
zero

you are beautiful
It is society
who is ugly

Marilyn Monroe

Often called "the Lady with the Lamp," **Florence Nightingale** (1820 – 1910) was a caring nurse and a leader. In addition to writing over 150 books, pamphlets and reports on health-related issues, she is also credited with creating one of the first versions of the pie chart. However, she is mostly known for making hospitals a cleaner and safer place to be.

Florence Nightingale was born in Florence, Italy even though both of her parents were English. Growing up in a wealthy family, Florence Nightingale was home-schooled by her father and expected to get married at a young age. However, when she was a teenager, Nightingale believed she received a "calling" from God to help the poor and the sick. Even though it was not a respected profession at the time, Nightingale told her parents that she wanted to become a nurse. Her parents did not approve of her decision and wanted her to get married and raise a family, but she refused. Eventually, her father allowed her to go to Germany to study nursing. After finishing there, she went to Paris for extra training with the Sisters of Mercy. By the time she was 33, Nightingale was already making a name for herself in the nursing community. She returned to England in 1853 and became the superintendent and manager of a hospital for "gentlewomen" in London.

When the Crimean War began in 1854, the British were unprepared to deal with the number of sick and injured soldiers. The lack of medical supplies, overcrowding, and unsanitary conditions caused many people to complain. Newspapers began to report about the terrible state of medical care and Florence Nightingale was asked to manage a group of nurses that would go and treat the wounded soldiers. She agreed, and on November 4, 1854, Nightingale and 38 nurses arrived at the British camp outside of Constantinople. When they got there, the doctors were unwelcoming because they did not want to work with female nurses. However, as the number of patients increased, the doctors needed their help. The nurses brought supplies, nutritious food, cleanliness, and sanitation to the military hospital. They also provided individual care and support. Within six months, Nightingale and her team transformed the hospital, and the death rate went down from 40 percent to 2 percent because of their work.

When Nightingale returned from the war, she continued to improve the conditions of hospitals. She presented her experiences and her data to Queen Victoria and Prince Albert in 1856. This data was the reason they formed a Royal Commission to improve the health of the British Army. Nightingale was so skilled with data and numbers that in 1858 she was also elected as the first woman member of the Royal Statistical Society and in 1859, she continued to spread her healthier medical practices by helping to set up the Army Medical College in Chatham. That same year, she published a book called *Notes on Nursing: What it is, and What it is Not*. Her book gives advice on good patient care and safe hospital environments. As a result of her efforts during the war, a fund was set up for Florence Nightingale to continue teaching nurses in England and in 1860, the Nightingale Training School at St. Thomas' Hospital was officially opened.

In her later years, Florence was often bedridden from illness, however, she continued to advocate for safe nursing practices until her death.

Although Florence Nightingale died on August 13th, 1910 at the age of 90, her legacy continues. Two years after her death, the International Committee of the Red Cross created the Florence Nightingale Medal that is presented to excellent nurses every two years. Also, International Nurses Day has been celebrated on her birthday since 1965.

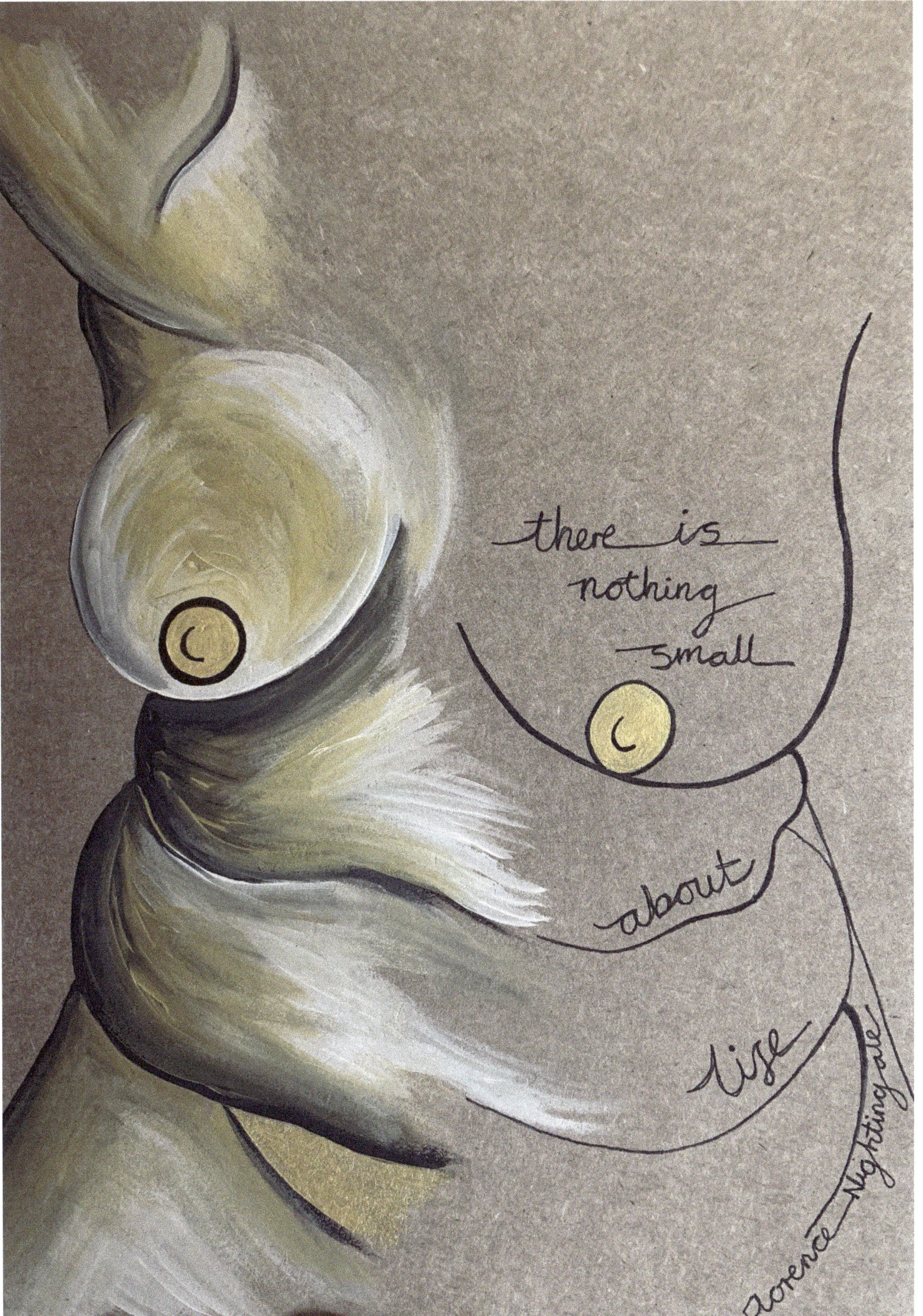

there is
nothing
small
about
life
Florence Nightingale

"Trust in God – She will provide."

Emmeline Pankhurst (1858 – 1928) was a British political activist. She is best remembered for organizing the UK suffragette movement and helping women win the right to vote.

Emmeline Goulden was born in Manchester into a family with a tradition of radical politics. A passionate and fearless campaigner for the rights of women, Emmeline declared herself a committed suffragist – a campaigner for women's right to vote – when she was just fourteen, and she went on to dedicate her life to the cause.

In 1879, she married Richard Pankhurst, a lawyer and supporter of the women's suffrage movement. He was the author of the Married Women's Property Acts of 1870 and 1882, which allowed women to keep earnings or property acquired before and after marriage. His death in 1898 was a great shock to Emmeline.

She fought tirelessly for the poor and oppressed, believing that society could only progress if women had an equal voice with men. In 1889, Emmeline founded the Women's Franchise League, which fought to allow married women to vote in local elections. In October 1903, she helped found the more militant Women's Social and Political Union (WSPU) – yet still continued a peaceful campaign for the vote. The motto of the WSPU was 'Deeds not words' but sadly, in the face of continued opposition, the suffragettes became more militant. They were soon an organisation that gained much notoriety for its activities and whose members were the first to be christened 'suffragettes.' Emmeline's daughters Christabel and Sylvia were both active in the cause. British politicians, press and public were astonished by the demonstrations, window smashing, arson and hunger strikes of the suffragettes. In 1913, WSPU member Emily Davison was killed when she threw herself under the king's horse at the Derby as a protest against the government's continued failure to grant women the right to vote.

Like many suffragettes, Emmeline was arrested on numerous occasions over the next few years and went on a hunger strike herself, resulting in violent force-feeding. In 1913, in response to the wave of hunger strikes, the government passed what became known as the 'Cat and Mouse' Act. Hunger striking prisoners were released until they grew strong again, and then re-arrested.

It wasn't until 1918 that the Representation of the People Act gave voting rights to women over 30 and then in 1928 the vote was given for women over 21.

Tragically, Emmeline died three weeks before the law was passed.

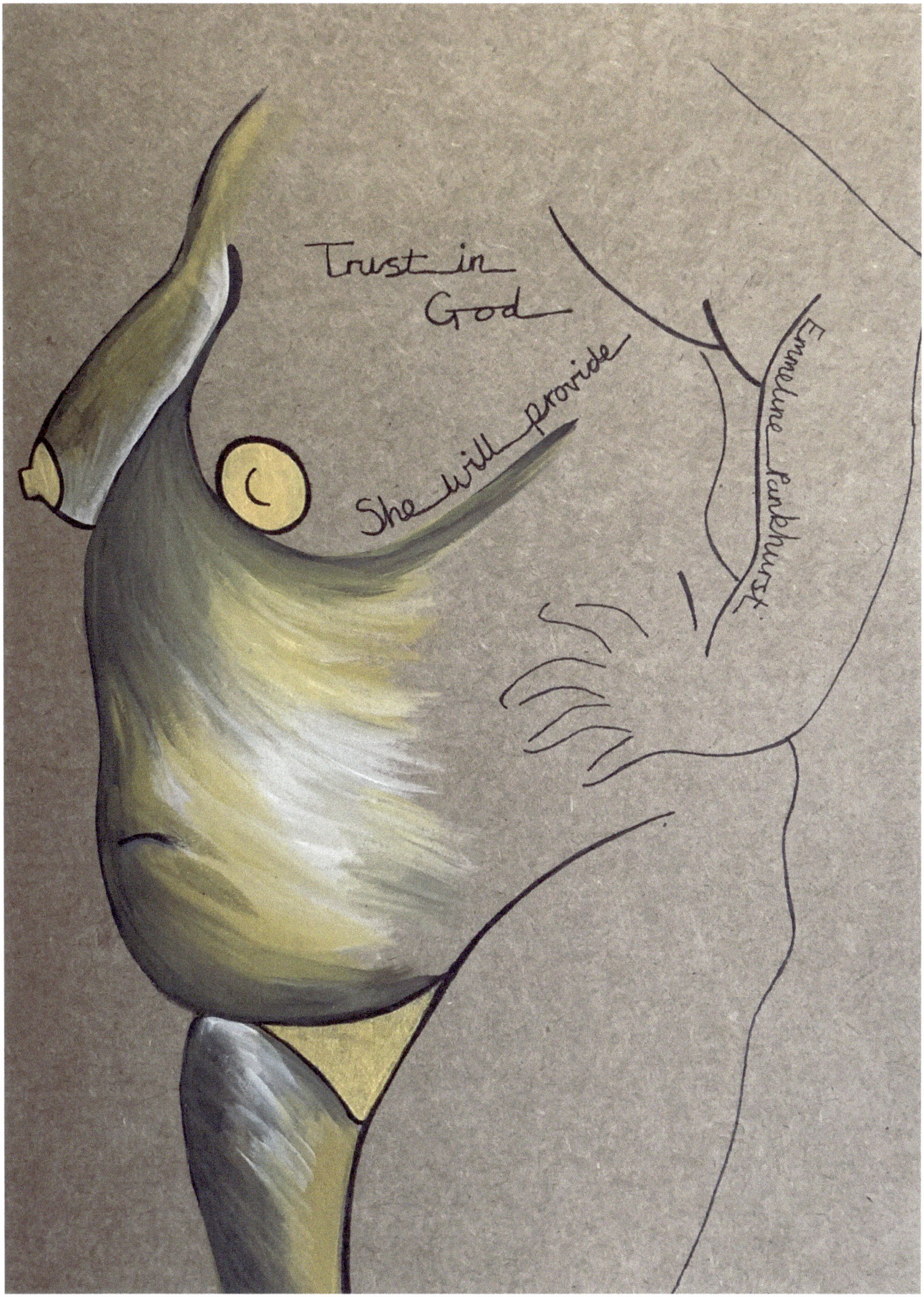

Trust in
God

She will provide

Emmeline Pankhurst

**"Be a first-rate version of yourself
rather than a second-rate version of someone else."**

Judy Garland (1922 – 1969) was an American actress, singer and dancer. She began her stage career as a child, attaining international stardom as an actress in both musical and dramatic roles – as a recording artist, and on the concert stage – in a career spanning 45 years.

Born Frances Ethel Gumm in Grand Rapids, Minnesota, Judy Garland was the star of many classic musical films, including *The Wizard of Oz*. She was known for her tremendous talent and troubled life. She signed a movie contract with MGM at the age of 13, appearing in the *Wizard of Oz* in 1939. She received a special Academy Award for her performance. She soon made several more musicals, including *Strike Up the Band* (1940), *Babes of Broadway* (1942), and *For Me and My Gal* (1943), with Gene Kelly.

It was around this time that her father died of spinal meningitis and Judy suffered tremendous heartache – the first of many to come. She married David Rose at the age of 19, but it was decidedly short-lived. She met director Vincent Minnelli on the set of *Meet Me in St. Louis* in 1944. She officially divorced Rose in 1945 and soon wed Minnelli, welcoming a daughter, Liza, in 1946. Unfortunately, Garland's second marriage only lasted a little longer than her first and they officially divorced in 1952.

Around this time, Judy began to break down emotionally. Exhausted from years of constant work and from all the medications she used to keep herself going, she developed a reputation for being unreliable and unstable – and was devastatingly dropped by MGM in 1950. Despite her personal anguish, Garland continued on her path to film stardom. In addition, due to her hectic work schedule, she was always under pressure from the studio about her looks and her weight. She was given amphetamines to boost her energy and control her weight. Unfortunately, Garland soon became reliant on this medication, along with other substances to help her sleep. Drug problems plagued her throughout the rest of her career.

In 1951, Garland started to rebuild her career with help from producer Sid Luft. She starred in her own show on Broadway at the Palace Theatre, earning a special Tony Award for her work on the show and her contributions to vaudeville in 1952. She married Luft in 1952, and they had two children together — daughter Lorna in 1952 and son Joey in 1955. Whatever personal difficulties Garland and Luft had, he had a positive impact on her career and was instrumental in putting together one of her greatest films.

Starring opposite James Mason, Garland gave an outstanding performance as a woman who obtains stardom at the price of love in *A Star Is Born* (1954) and she was nominated for an Academy Award.

On June 22, 1969, Judy Garland died in London of what was reported to be an accidental overdose. Despite the highs and lows of the life of an icon – Judy Garland was woman who definitely made HERstory.

be a first
rate version
of yourself
rather than
a second
rate version of
someone else
Judy Garland

**"They say I am a savage and dangerous woman.
I am speaking the truth and the truth is savage and dangerous."**

Nawal El Saadawi (1931 — 2021) was an Egyptian feminist writer, activist, physician, and psychiatrist. She wrote many books on the subject of women in Islam, paying particular attention to the practice of female genital mutilation in her society. Born in the village of Kafr Tahla, just north of Cairo, the second of nine children, Nawal el Saadawi was encouraged to study.

Her first dream was to be a dancer; she loved music and she was beautiful. But her father could not afford a piano, so she turned her attention instead to reading and writing. She never wanted to be a doctor, but as she was top of her class, it was almost automatic and she got a scholarship. She graduated from the University of Cairo in 1955, specialising in psychiatry, returning to Kafr Tahla to work as a doctor. In 1972, she published *Women and Sex*, the first of a series of books in which she attacked the aggressions carried out against women's bodies; not just female circumcision, but also the brutal rituals associated with society's fixation with virginity. The same dayas [midwives] who circumcised children were often required to prove a girl's hymen was intact on her wedding night. Soon after this, she lost her job– and *al-Sihha* [Health], the magazine she had founded three years previously, was closed down.

She continued to write – *Woman at Point Zero* was published in 1973, and *The Hidden Face of Eve* in 1977 – and the state continued to make her life difficult. It was inevitable that they would one day come for her, and eventually they did. At the prison, she shared a cell with 12 other women, and was smuggled in an eye pencil, which enabled her to write her memoirs on toilet paper. She had a feeling that everything would be all right – and so it proved.

After 3 marriages, she said "I'm telling you frankly: I am not really fit for the role of a wife, you must be sure of that."

In Egypt, her supporters established a Nawal El Saadawi forum, which holds regular meetings in Cairo and elsewhere at which her books are discussed at some length. El Saadawi published more than 50 titles in Arabic during her lifetime. The international awards continue to pile up, as did the invitations to speak about several of her most important books – among them the novel *Woman at Point Zero*, which tells the story of Firdaus, a victim of sexual abuse who awaits execution in a Cairo prison cell, and *The Hidden Face of Eve*, her classic analysis of female oppression in the Arab world. Among its pages is a taboo-breaking description of El Saadawi's circumcision at the age of six, an operation that was performed on the floor of the family bathroom while her mother looked on, laughing and smiling.

Her opinion was much in demand until her death on March 21, 2021. She was entirely fearless, striding where others still fear to tread.

they say I am
a savage and
dangerous woman

I am
speaking
the truth

and the truth is
savage and
dangerous

Nawal el Saadawi

Mary Wollstonecraft (1759 – 1797) was an English writer, philosopher, and advocate of women's rights. Mary was born into prosperity but her alcoholic father squandered the family money. Like her mother, she often suffered abuse at his hands. While her older brother, Ned, received an extensive formal education, Mary spent just a few years in a day school. The discrepancy infuriated her. Why should she be denied the opportunities afforded to her brother just because she was a girl? She resolved, with characteristic determination, to educate herself.

In her best-selling book *A Vindication of the Rights of Woman*, Wollstonecraft took the principles of the revolution to their logical conclusion, outlining a vision of equality between the sexes. If women were afforded the same opportunities and education, she wrote, they could contribute as much to society as men.

Like many prominent reformers, Mary left for Paris and was embraced by the radicals shaping a new social order in France. She met the American, Gilbert Imlay, and defying moral convention, they became lovers, resulting the birth of her first child, Fanny, out of wedlock. The relationship proved both short-lived and devastating for Mary. She found out Imlay was having an affair, but she was desperate to save the relationship – only to find out he had betrayed her again. Distraught, she threw herself off Putney Bridge into the Thames – only to be saved by the intervention of passing watermen.

Wollstonecraft emerged from the depths of her despair and found personal happiness with an unlikely partner. William Godwin was a famous radical philosopher who Wollstonecraft first met at a dinner held by her publisher in 1791. They fell in love. Although Godwin was opposed to the principle of marriage, when Wollstonecraft fell pregnant, they wed in March 1797. Despite being married, the couple maintained an unconventional domestic arrangement, living in two homes and communicating through notes.

On 30 August, Wollstonecraft went into labour. After about 18 hours she gave birth to her second child, a daughter, also named Mary. But there were minor complications which the surgeon mishandled and she suffered acute haemorrhaging and infection. Sadly, she died after 11 days at the young age of 38.

Today Wollstonecraft is widely recognised as a principal figure in the fight for sexual equality and her work is still published around the world. The ebbs and flows of Wollstonecraft's reputation are inextricably tied to society's wider view of women's rights. Her rehabilitation has been championed by some of the most preeminent feminists of the 20th Century, including suffragist leader Millicent Fawcett and Virginia Woolf. By the time the bicentenary edition of *Rights of Woman* was published, Mary was an established feminist icon. Today she remains an enduring symbol of the ongoing fight against misogyny.

Mary Wollstonecraft

The beginning

is always today

"Tell your own story."

Louise Joséphine Bourgeois (1911 – 2010) was a French-American artist who explored patriarchy, motherhood and what it meant for women to be subjects, rather than objects, of art. With a career spanning eight decades from the 1930s until 2010, Louise Bourgeois is one of the great figures of modern and contemporary art. She is best known for her large-scale sculptures and installations that are inspired by her own memories and experiences. Bourgeois was also a prolific painter and printmaker.

Themes of domestic life, motherhood, domesticity and the home reoccur throughout Louise Bourgeois's work, as well as sexuality and feeling lost and trapped as a woman. She explores the role of female identity throughout every piece of art – often challenging the conventional role of women in the twentieth century. This is what has led her to become synonymous with the feminist art movement, taking on an almost ambassadorial role. She was a strong feminist, but never called herself a 'female artist' or a 'feminist artist' as she believed that to call her such is reductive – she was dealing with universal emotions: jealousy, rejection, and so on, and these are pre-gender. It wasn't that she explicitly rejected being defined in feminist terms ("Some of my works are, or try to be feminist, and others are not feminist," she once said in an interview with the San Francisco Museum of Art). Rather, she adopted a contrary attitude towards critics eager to pigeonhole her exclusively with those terms.

"Spider" was one of her most famous series of works – in 1947 Louise Bourgeois drew two small ink and charcoal drawings of a spider. Fifty years later, in the late 1990s, she created a series of steel and bronze spider sculptures. "The spider is an ode to my mother. She was my best friend. Like a spider, my mother was a weaver… Like spiders, my mother was very clever. Spiders are friendly presences that eat mosquitos. We know that mosquitos spread diseases and are therefore unwanted. So, spiders are helpful and protective, just like my mother. I came from a family of repairers. The spider is a repairer. If you bash into the web of a spider, she does not get mad. She weaves and repairs it."

Bourgeois uses the spider – both predator (a sinister threat) and protector (an industrious repairer) – to symbolise the mother figure. The spider showed women as protectors: strong, maternal and powerful – Bourgeois's nod to the unbalanced patriarchal systems and showing the power of women.

Just as she seemed to find her feet in the 1950s, the male-dominated genre of abstract expressionism exploded, making stars of male contemporaries such as Jackson Pollock and Mark Rothko, and overshadowing her sculptures. She began, through her work, to rebel against the patriarchy this represented – because her opinion was that the surrealists made women the object of their work, whereas she was trying to make women the subject.

Tell your own story
Louise Bourgeois

***"I have been absolutely terrified every moment of my life —
and I have never let it keep me from doing a single thing."***

Georgia Totto O'Keeffe (1887 – 1986) was an American artist who was known primarily for her paintings of enlarged flowers. O'Keeffe has been recognized as the "Mother of American modernism" and is also considered by some to be the foremother of the feminist art movement. She worked in a discipline dominated by male artists, critics, gallery owners, and curators, who were all critical of women artists. Yet despite these obstacles, O'Keeffe launched a successful career, developing a distinctive painting style that employed organic vulvar forms and floral imagery.

She was raised on a farm in Wisconsin and took art lessons from a very young age. Encouraged by her teachers, she graduated high school with the goal of becoming an artist. She attended the Art Institute of Chicago for one year and studied at the Art Students League in New York City, where the dominant emphasis was on realism, an artistic method representing people, places, and things as true to their appearance. In 1908, her last year with the League, she won the William Merritt Chase still life prize for her painting Untitled (Dead Rabbit with Copper Pot). She then quit painting for four years, claiming later that it was due to her frustration with the tradition she was working in.

In 1912, at a summer course for art teachers, Georgia came across the teaching that the artist's goal was to express his/her own thoughts and feelings. This provided O'Keeffe with an alternative to the type of realism she had been trained in.

Inspired, she began painting again. While working as an art teacher in South Carolina in 1915, O'Keeffe began a series of abstract charcoal paintings. She mailed them to a former classmate in New York, who took them to a celebrated photographer and owner of the well-known gallery "291" – who exhibited O'Keeffe's work. With his financial assistance, she moved to New York and they fell in love shortly after. They married in 1924. During their marriage, the well-connected Stieglitz promoted O'Keeffe's work, particularly the close-ups of flowers that she began producing in the mid-1920s. She had numerous one-woman gallery exhibitions, and her first retrospective, *Paintings by Georgia O'Keeffe*, opened at the Brooklyn Museum in 1927. Her husband died in 1946, and three years later O'Keeffe moved to New Mexico, drawn by its vibrant colours and the unique landscape formations.

She was awarded the Medal of Freedom in 1977, as well as the National Medal of Arts in 1985. Although her poor eyesight forced her to stop painting in the 1970s, she continued to work in pencil, watercolor, and clay until her health worsened in 1984. She died in 1986, at the age of ninety-eight. Since the 1920s her work has become more popular, due, in part, to the feminist movement and its reclamation and rediscovery of women's history. In talking about her work, O'Keeffe said, "The men liked to put me down as the best woman painter. I think I'm one of the best painters." The Georgia O'Keeffe Museum, the first museum in the United States dedicated to a single female artist, opened in 1997 in Santa Fe, New Mexico. It houses 1,149 of her works.

I have been
terrified every moment
of my life
and I
have never
let it keep me
from doing
a single
thing
Georgia O'Keeffe

"Well behaved woman seldom make history."

This is a much-loved quote, and is attributed to Eleanor Roosevelt, Anne Boleyn, Marilyn Monroe and
Laurel Thatcher Ulrich. Research shows, however, that the earliest evidence of this quote appeared in
an academic paper in the journal "American Quarterly" in 1976. The others have repeated the quote,
changing the word seldom to "rarely" or "never."

Laurel Thatcher Ulrich (born in 1938) is a Pulitzer Prize-winning American historian specializing
in early America and the history of women. She is also a professor at Harvard University. In 1976, she
was a student of the University of New Hampshire and earned her Ph.D. in history in 1980. The goal of
most of her work was the recovery of the history of women who were not featured in history books of
the past. She was interested in portraying more fully the lives of ordinary women who were considered
"well-behaved" or "virtuous" – looking where others didn't to highlight "lost" women.

She says: "History is essential to many movements for social change. If you believe that things have
always been the way they are now, you don't have a history – because history is the study of how
things change over time. But if you can investigate history, and begin to rewrite history, then you have
a different orientation toward the future. History is our job. If we just sit and passively accept our own
circumstances, nothing will change. So: well-behaved women seldom make history."

As a feminist scholar, Ulrich has made history herself. Her second book, *A Midwife's Tale: The Life of
Martha Ballard*, won the Pulitzer Prize in History – the first book of women's history to receive the
prize. Ballard's diary was full of references to the household production of cloth, and it occurred to
Ulrich that there was a story to be told there, as well. She published *The Age of Homespun: Objects
and Stories in the Creation of an American Myth*, examining early American history through 14
domestic objects: not just fabric, but tools such as baskets and spinning wheels, and furniture. When
women handed down household goods to their daughters, there was no legal record. Histories of
these objects "had to be teased out of provenance records in museums, where you could see where
something came from and how it survived over time," she says. "That taught me a lot about what I
would call 'female lines of inheritance.'"

Ulrich's new book is *A House Full of Females: Plural Marriage and Women's Rights in Early
Mormonism, 1835–1870* examines female activism – women secured the vote in Utah half a century
before the passage of the 19th Amendment – and the marriage system, using artifacts such as diaries,
ledgers, meeting notes, and quilts.

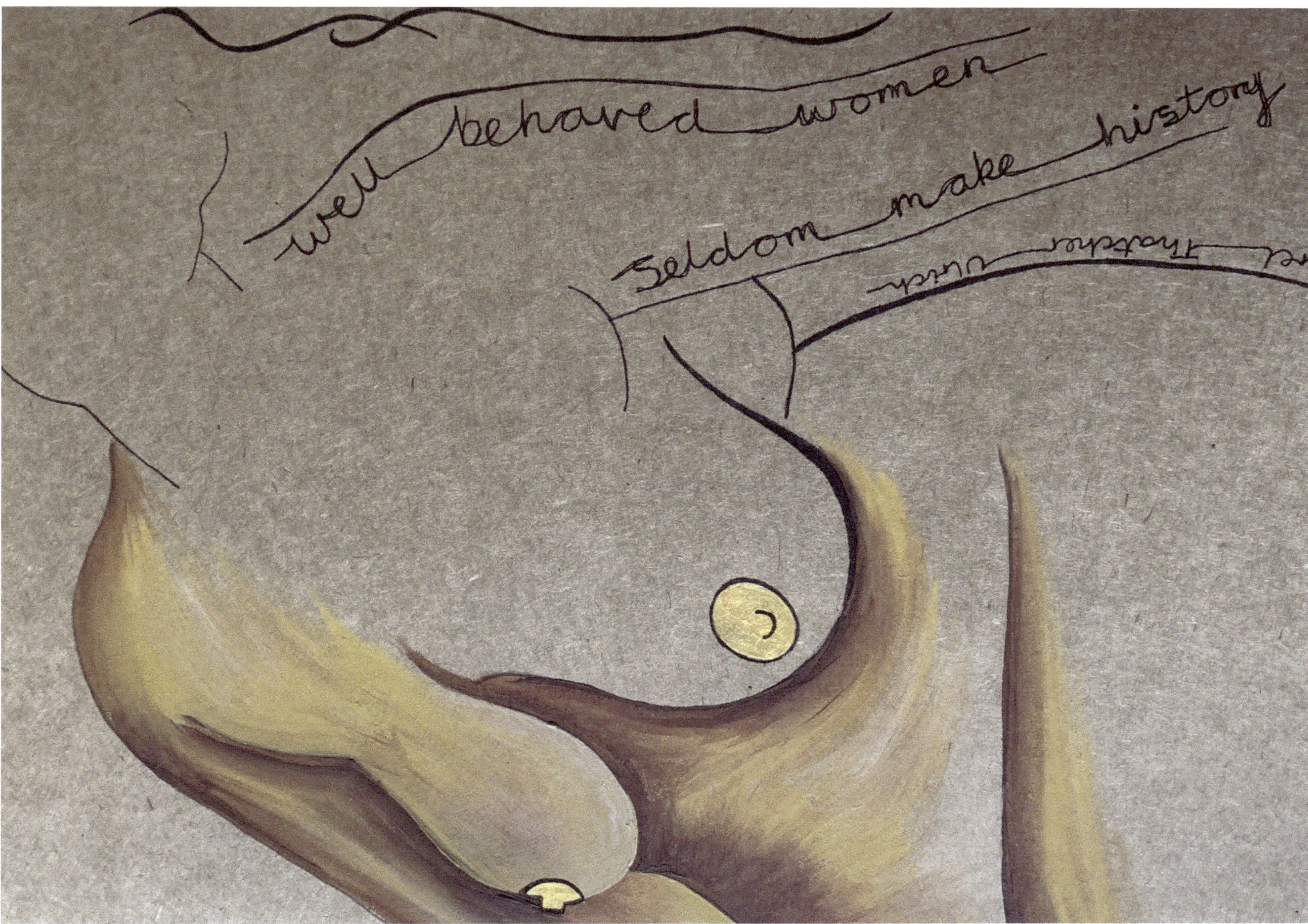

well behaved women
Seldom make history
rel Thatcher which

"Through the study of women, you get to the heart and truth of culture."

Iranian contemporary visual artist and filmmaker, **Shirin Neshat** (born 26th March 1957) gives us a unique lens into the contradictions within Islamic feminism. She uses her situation as a culturally-hybrid individual to mediate the contradiction between Eastern and Western cultures and male and female relationships.

Even beyond the Middle East, Shirin Neshat is a household name in the contemporary art world. Working across film, photography and video, she arguably first achieved international acclaim with _Rapture_ (1999), which addresses the relationship between women and the cultural value system of Islam. Born in 1957 in Qazin, Iran, Neshat left to study at the University of California at Berkeley, on the cusp of the Iranian Revolution in 1979. Her earlier work, the _Women of Allah_ series, looks at the intersections of gender, identity and society – particularly poignant at a time when Middle Eastern (and especially Iranian) society disintegrated under the politics of war. Her split-screened video _Turbulent_ (1998) won the First International Prize at the Venice Biennale and she later won the Silver Lion for best director. Since then, her work has earned major exhibitions at MoMA and the Tate Modern among others. _Huffington Post_ has named her Artist of the Decade.

Famous filmmaker Maryam Keshavarz says of Neshat "I love her work, she's operating on another level. I remember seeing _Rapture_ and thinking 'Oh my god here's a woman who is not living in Iran but taking those memories and visualizing them, sounding them; that is so visceral and moving beyond the narrative.'"

Neshat's contribution to the contemporary art world is undeniable and still continues to be politically relevant. However, she is not just concerned with contemporary politics. Neshat's historical awareness has recently taken a revisionist position – as shown in her most recent film _Looking for Oum Kulthum_ (2018), where she outlines an agenda to rewrite women into dominant historical narratives within Middle Eastern culture.

Through the
study of women

You get to
the heart
and truth
of culture

Shirin Neshat

"The truth will set you free, but first it will piss you off."

From her humble Ohio childhood, **Gloria Steinem** grew up to become an acclaimed journalist, trailblazing feminist, and one of the most visible, passionate leaders and spokeswomen of the women's rights movement in the late 20th and early 21st centuries.

Steinem was born on March 25, 1934 in Toledo, Ohio — the second child and daughter of Leo and Ruth Steinem. Her father worked as a traveling salesman. In 1944, her parents divorced, leaving a young Steinem to take care of her mentally ill mother in Toledo. After graduating high school, her sister came to care for their mother, and Steinem attended Smith College in Massachusetts where she studied government. She graduated and then spent two years studying and researching in India. Her time abroad inspired an interest in grassroots activism, which would later manifest itself in her work with the Women's Liberation Movement and the Equal Rights Amendment.

Steinem started her professional career as a journalist in New York, writing freelance pieces for various publications – which was tough for women in the late 1950s and 1960s, when men ran the newsrooms and women were largely relegated to secretarial and behind-the-scenes research roles. Steinem's early articles tended to focus on what was then called "the women's pages," lifestyle or service features about such female-centred or fashion topics as nylon stockings. Steinem once recalled that, "When I suggested political stories to _The New York Times Sunday Magazine_, my editor just said something like, 'I don't think of you that way.'" Undeterred, Steinem pushed on, seeking more substantial social and political reporting assignments. She gained national attention in 1963 when _Show_ magazine hired her to go undercover to report on the working conditions at Hugh Hefner's Playboy Club.

In 1970, feminist activists staged a take-over of _Ladies Home Journal,_ arguing that the magazine only offered articles on housekeeping but failed to cover women's rights and the women's movement. Steinem soon realized the value of a women's movement magazine and joined forces with journalists Patricia Carbine and Letty Cottin Pogrebin to found _Ms. Magazine_. It debuted in 1971 as an insert in _New York_ magazine. In 1972, _Ms._ became an independent, regular circulation magazine. Steinem remained an editor and writer for the magazine for the next fifteen years and continues to support it to the present.

Steinem's life has been dedicated to the cause of women's rights, as she led marches and toured the country as an in-demand speaker. In 1972, Steinem and feminists such as Congresswoman Bella Abzug, Congresswoman Shirley Chisholm, and feminist Betty Friedan formed the National Women's Political Caucus. It continues to support gender equality and to ensure the election of more pro-equality women to public office.

Other organizations Steinem has co-founded during her vast career include the Women's Action Alliance (1971), which promotes non-sexist, multi-racial children's education; the Women's Media Center (2004) to promote positive images of women in media; Voters for Choice (1977), a prochoice political action committee; and the Ms. Foundation for Women. In the 1990s, she helped establish Take Our Daughters to Work Day, the first national effort to empower young girls to learn about career opportunities.

In 2000, at age 66, the long-single Steinem married for the first time in a Cherokee ceremony in Oklahoma. Her husband, entrepreneur and activist David Bale, sadly died of lymphoma four years later.

An award-winning and prolific writer, Steinem has authored several books, including a biography on Marilyn Monroe, and the best-selling _My Life on the Road_. Her work has also been published and reprinted in numerous anthologies and textbooks. In 2013, President Barack Obama presented her with the Presidential Medal of Freedom, the highest civilian honour.

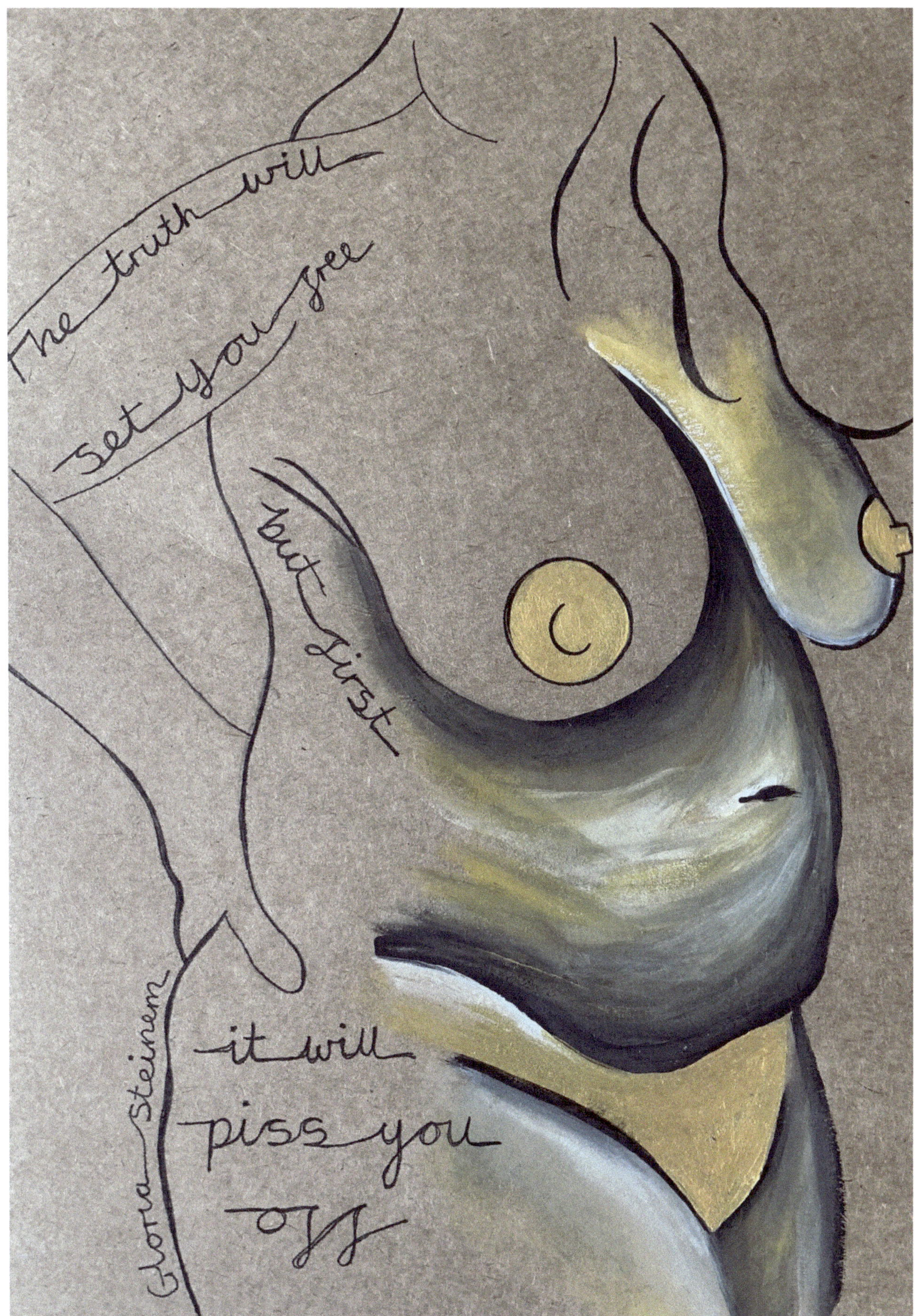

The truth will
set you free
but first
it will
piss you
off
Gloria Steinem

"For most of history, anonymous was a woman."

Adeline Virginia Woolf (1882 – 1941) was an extremely important female author, and before her death at the age of 59, she published several novels and feminist essays.

She was an outsider for her incredibly free vision of women in society and was a pioneer of the early twentieth century feminism. With her job as journalist and writer, she increased the self-confidence of many women during the Nineteenth century.

Born as the third child of Sir Leslie Stephen, the editor of the _Dictionary of National Biography_, and his second wife Julia Duckworth, Virginia and her siblings grew up in London where she always had easy access to education, including private classes in Latin and Greek – which was not common for girls in Victorian times – and also to her father's library.

Her mother's death in 1895 and, seven years later, her father's death of cancer affected Virginia greatly. After traveling to Spain, she returned to London and got married in 1912 to Leonard Woolf.

In 1918, Leonard and Virginia Woolf published the first edition of Virginia's short story "Key Garden," followed by many books, including _To the Lighthouse_ (1927) and _A Room of One's Own_ (1929). They printed the _Hogarth Press_ in their own house in London.

She had almost finished her last novel _Between the Acts_ when her mental state became more and more unstable. She sadly drowned herself in a river in Sussex.

Virginia Woolf wrote about the detriments caused by gender-influenced salaries long before moves were made to change legislation. In _A Room of One's Own_, she famously explains that without financial freedom, women cannot possess full creative or intellectual freedom. While Woolf's essay directly evaluates the role of education – withheld from many women of her time – she goes on to equate schooling with income and self-sufficiency. She says, "Take no advice, follow your own instincts, use your own reason, come to your own conclusions."

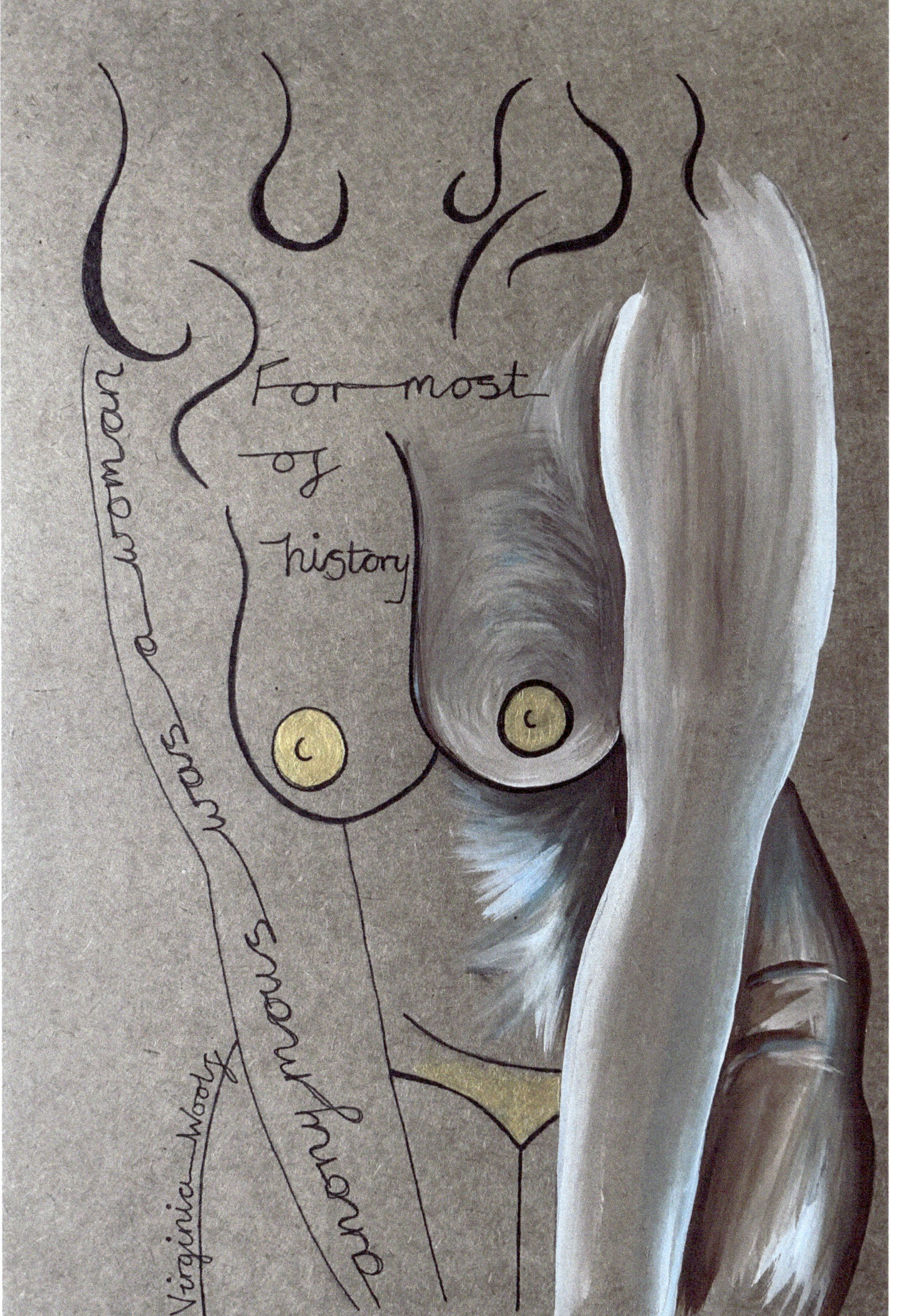
For most of history
anonymous was a woman
Virginia Woolf

"Free thinking, powerful, passionate women are dangerous to a conservative male-dominated culture. They tend to do what they want."

Lucy H. Pearce, 41, is a total inspiration. Not only for her ground-breaking writing and soul-healing empowerment books – but because she is a real-life woman, living fearlessly in this woman-hating-world. She has stepped up single-handedly to society, offering the giant middle finger to the patriarchal paradigms that bind women to lives less worthy than their magnificence – and for that she needs to be applauded.

Lucy is here. Now. Shouting and being heard and making the world sit up and listen. A modern-day woman that we can all look to for encouragement, motivation and insight as we step into our own power and Divine Feminine strength. She lives and breathes the creative rainbow mother archetype in a little pink house on the south coast of Ireland in the town of her birth – and is an established writer, editor, artist, women's workshop facilitator and mother of three teenage children.

She is the author of multiple life-changing non-fiction books for women, including her best-selling – *Burning Woman* – an incendiary exploration of women and power – written for every woman who burns with passion, has been burned with shame, and in another time or place would be burned at the stake. I think we can all relate to that!

Her other pivotal books include *Medicine Woman: Reclaiming the Soul of Healing*, *Creatrix: she who makes,* and her latest incredible offering: *She of the Sea* – a deep dive into the ocean, exploring where women meet the salty, sacred magic.

She has also contributed to a number of book anthologies. Her words and artwork have been featured in magazines, diaries and calendars all over the world – empowering women every step of the way, and she blogs creatively at *Dreaming Aloud*.

Lucy's work is dedicated to supporting women's empowered, embodied expression through her writing, teaching and art. She runs Womancraft Publishing – creating life-changing, paradigm-shifting books by women, for women. She is a total advocate for pushing women, as she does herself, to reach their highest and fullest potential, healing all whose lives she touches with her creativity along the way.

Lucy says: "Our communities – global and local are hungry for people of vision, projects of hope, people standing fully in their power and not dominated by fear. We need to find the courage to harness our greatest visions and live them out. We need to embody our values. Dare to live authentically. Risk vulnerability. Face down shame, repression and taboo. Dreaming new dreams not only for ourselves but for the entire human race. Each of our voices matter so much."

As a late diagnosed autistic woman who has openly struggled with her anxiety, Lucy is even more of an inspiration to all, saying "Without the fear and the shame, I would not have had the fire and creative impetus."

Lucy H Pearce has not made HERstory – she is MAKING HERstory right now!

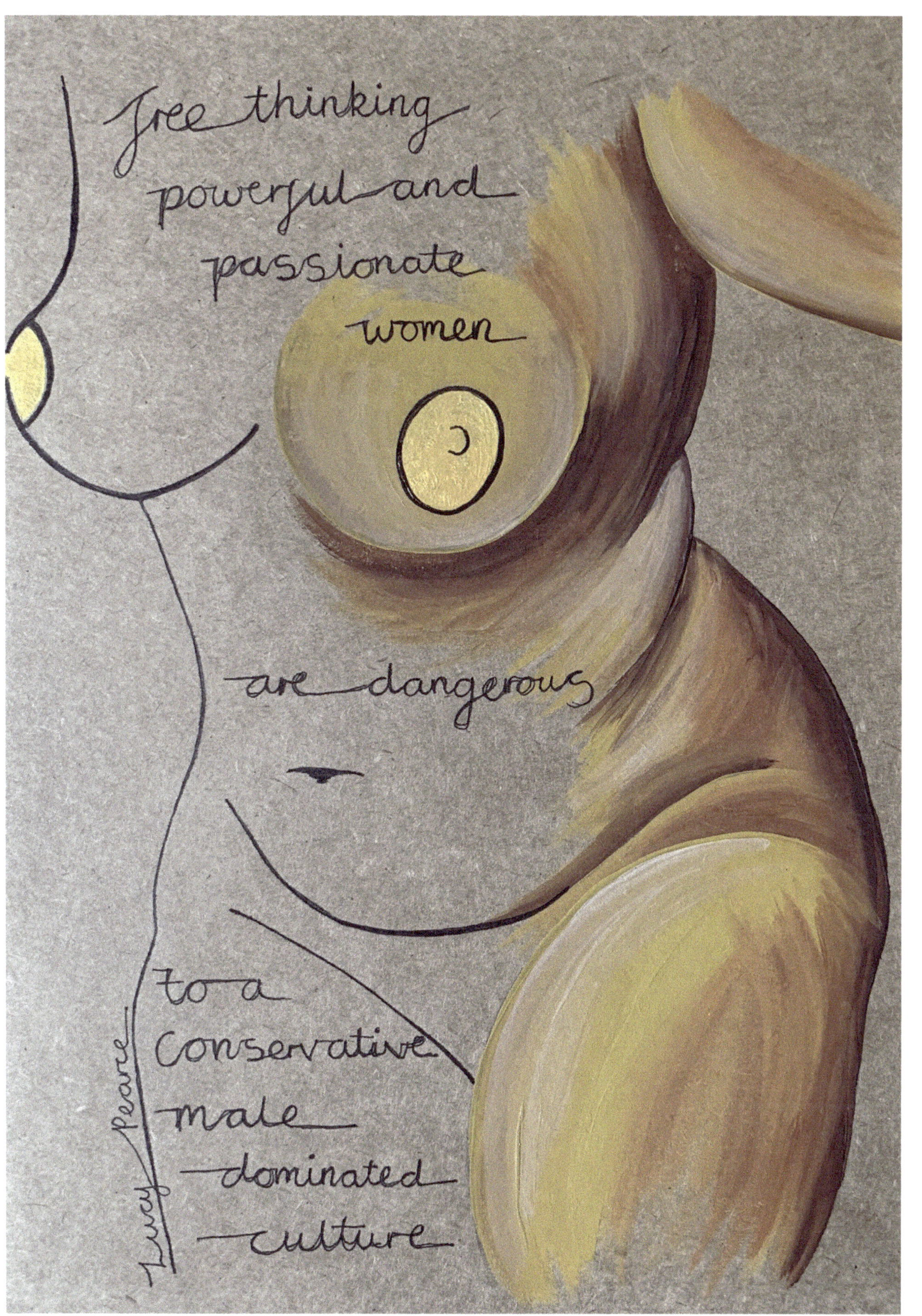

free thinking
powerful and
passionate
women
are dangerous
to a
conservative
male
dominated
culture
Lucy Pearce

"My misfortune has turned out to be my greatest blessing."

Annette Marie Sarah Kellermann (1886 – 1975) was born in New South Wales, Australia. She was just 6 years old when she developed weakness in her legs, requiring her to wear painful steel braces. To help her rehabilitate, her parents enrolled her into swimming classes at Cavill's Baths, a tidal swimming pool in the North Sydney suburb of Lavender Bay. By the age of 13, her legs were practically normal, and by 15, she had mastered all the swimming strokes and won her first race. At this time she was also giving diving displays and swimming exhibitions, performing mermaid acts and doing two shows a day swimming with fish in a glass tank at the Exhibition Aquarium. Soon, she became a champion swimmer – a record holder in the ladies' 100 yards and mile championships of New South Wales in the record times of 1 minute, 22 seconds and 33 minutes, 49 seconds respectively. But more than just swimming, she became famous for advocating women's rights.

Annette Kellerman was never going to conform to society. A trailblazing Australian swimmer turned Hollywood vaudeville star, she held all the world records for women's swimming in 1905 and appeared in several movies, usually with aquatic themes. As the star of _A Daughter of the Gods_, was the first major actress to appear nude in a Hollywood production. She also helped popularize the sport of synchronised swimming, authored a swimming manual and was an advocate of health, fitness, and natural beauty throughout her life. She also performed her own stunts, including a 20-metre dive into the ocean with her hands and feet bound, and jumping into a pool of crocodiles.

In the early 1900s, women swam in black, knee-length wool dresses worn over bloomers with long black stockings, bathing slippers, and even ribboned swim caps. But in 1907, Kellerman stepped out onto Revere Beach, Boston, wearing a one-piece bathing suit that ended in shorts above her knees. It caused a huge scandal. Police were called, and she was arrested for indecency. She was quoted as saying: "I can't swim wearing more stuff than you hang on a clothes-line."

This led to her becoming an advocate for women's bodies, which have long been a political battleground, subject to legislation and regulation. Swimwear was a particularly controversial area and in the USA at that time, policemen measured women's swimsuits on the beach as modesty laws demanded shorts were no more than six inches above the knee.

When Kellerman rejected the heavy, cumbersome woollen pantaloons women were expected to wear at the beach, she was sending a powerful message about female autonomy, choice and freedom: Be who you are, wear what you want! She went on to design her own line of one-piece bathing suits, keeping her fight alive, and with time, she helped change the social norms and the one-piece suit became a popular swimsuit for women.

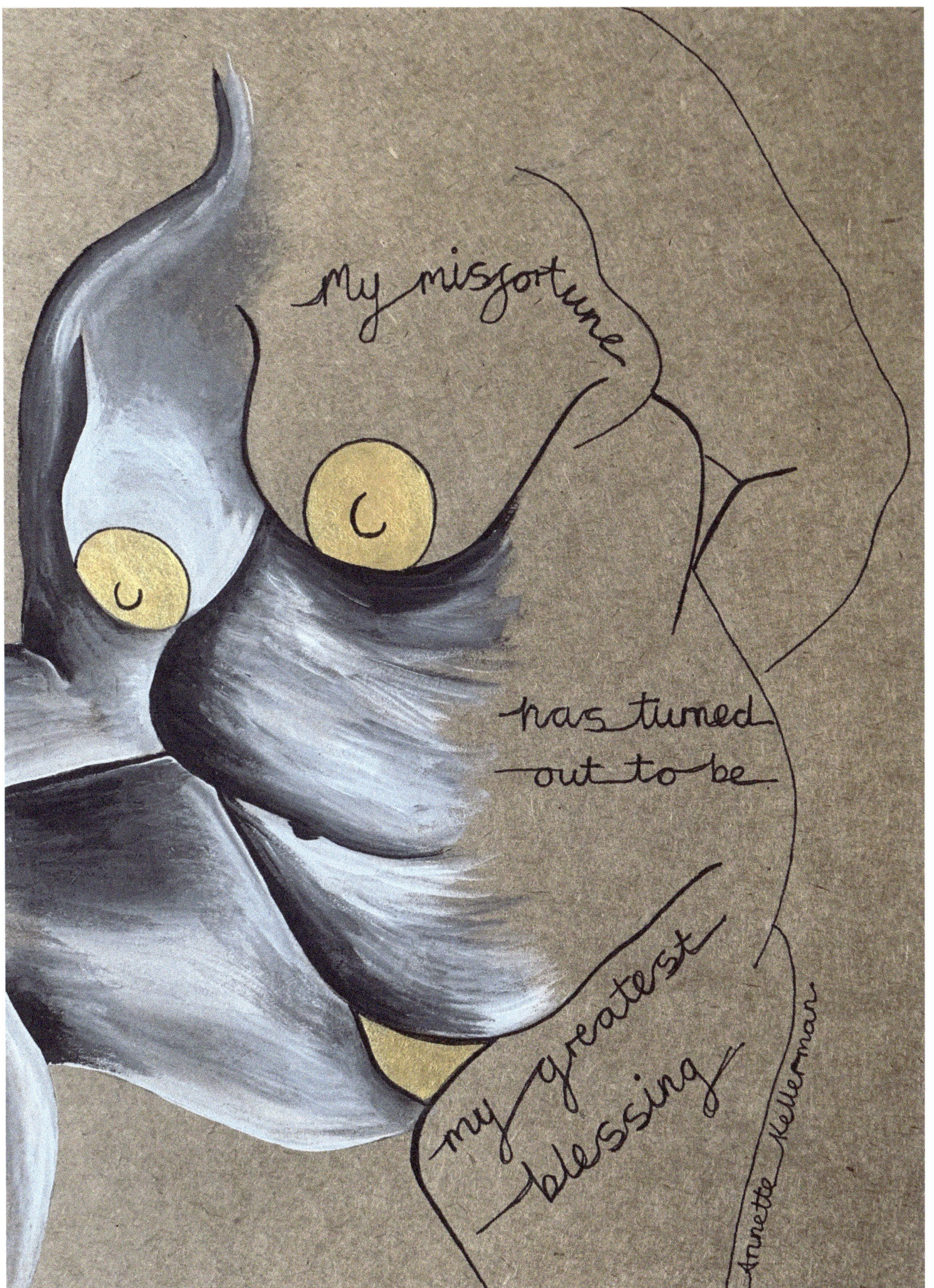

My missfortune
has turned
out to be
my greatest
blessing
Annette Kellerman.

**"And the day came when the risk it took to remain tight in the bud
was more painful that the risk it took to blossom."**

Angela Anaïs Juana Antolina Rosa Edelmira Nin y Culmell (1903 – 1977), known professionally as Anaïs Nin, was a French-Cuban American diarist, essayist, novelist and writer of short stories and erotica, embodying the practice of writing as a path to delving deeply into herself.

Her father, Joaquin Nin, a composer, deserted the family when Anaïs was about 11 years old. Anaïs spent her teens in the U.S., starting out in Catholic school. She then dropped out, became self-educated, and worked as a model and dancer before returning to Europe in the 1920s.

In her lifetime, Nin caused controversy for many differing reasons, possibly mainly for being a woman who wrote explicitly about sex from a female point of view, included frank portrayals of illegal abortions, extramarital affairs and incest – all of which she wrote about without judging her female characters. Writing of that nature and the imaginative and unheard of erotic stories she produced would be brave in today's age, but in 1940, it was described as "career suicide!"

She also believed that she was by far her most fascinating character, and that her diaries ought to be treated as a major work of literature – but this was misinterpreted, leading to her being accused of narcissism, sociopathy and sexual perversion time and again. One memorable headline labelled her as "a monster of self-centeredness whose artistic pretensions seem grotesque."

But Nin was the first of her kind. And, like all truly unique talents, she was worshipped by some, hated by many, and misunderstood by most. Above all, she refused to change or be moulded to fit in or be accepted and liked. Much to her delight, *The Diary of Anaïs Nin* was finally published in 1966 – a monumental life's work that Nin completed in secret – spanning seven volumes and 50 years. Reviews were surprisingly amazing considering that until that moment she was generally viewed as an unfashionable, underground author receiving almost no attention from the mainstream press. Sales also surpassed expectations.

She began writing the Diaries in 1931 – and her personal quest for self-knowledge ended up becoming an in-depth, honest look at the universal issues affecting women in all walks of life. "It's all right for a woman to be, above all, human. I am a woman first of all," she wrote.

Published during the 1960s and 1970s – when she herself was in her sixties and seventies – the Diary series hit a nerve and was a success from the start. In the final volume of the Diaries, she delights in sharing her reaction to the positive feedback it got: "Having been told so often how wrong it is to write about one's self—how I should take the self out of the Diary – I never expected the consequences. Because I gave of myself, many women felt I spoke for them, liberated them from secrecy and reticence. I did not expect to get letters from women working in offices, on farms, married and lonely in little towns, nurses, librarians, students, runaways, dropouts, pregnant women without husbands, women in the middle of a divorce. Suddenly I was discovering a world of women. The dominant theme of the letters was loneliness and lack of confidence in whatever the writers undertook. The miracle was that my diary made them eloquent, confessional… I discovered women with talents never used before. One woman sent me her first drawing made after reading the Diary. The Diary cured depression and opened secret chambers. There was no ego in the Diary, there was only a voice which spoke for thousands, made links, bonds, friendships. All the clichés about self-absorption were destroyed. There was no one self. We were all one. The more I developed myself, the less mine it became. If all of us were willing to expose this self, we would not feel alone." -Anaïs Nin, from *The Diary of Anaïs Nin, Volume Seven, 1966-1974*

And so began the age of Anaïs Nin, feminist icon: Worshipped by young women who believed she had provided the first real account of how a woman could thrive in the male-dominated world of literature.

and the
day came
when the risk
it took
to remain tight
in the bud
was more painful than
the risk it took
to blossom
Anaïs Nin

**"There shall never be another season of silence until women
have the same rights as men on this green earth."**

Susan B. Anthony (1820 – 1906) was an American social reformer and women's rights activist who played a pivotal role in the women's suffrage movement. Born into a Quaker family committed to social equality, she collected anti-slavery petitions at the age of 17.

Champion of abolition and equal pay for equal work, Susan Brownell Anthony became one of the most visible leaders of the women's suffrage movement. Along with Elizabeth Cady Stanton, she travelled around the country delivering speeches in favour of women's suffrage.

She was born on February 15th in Adams, Massachusetts. Her father, Daniel, was a farmer and later a cotton mill owner and manager. Her mother, Lucy, came from a family that fought in the American Revolution and served in the Massachusetts state government. From an early age, she was inspired by her family's Quaker belief that everyone was equal under God. That idea guided her throughout her life – as it did her seven brothers and sisters, many of whom became activists for justice and emancipation of slaves.

After many years of teaching, Susan B Anthony returned to her family who had moved to New York State. There she met William Lloyd Garrison and Frederick Douglass, who were friends of her father. Listening to them moved Susan to want to do more to help end slavery. She became an abolition activist, even though most people thought it was improper for women to give speeches in public. Anthony made many passionate speeches against slavery.

In 1848, a group of women held a convention at Seneca Falls, New York. It was the first Women's Rights Convention in the United States and began the Suffrage movement. Her mother and sister attended the convention, but Susan did not.

In 1851, Anthony met Elizabeth Cady Stanton. The two women became good friends and worked together for over 50 years fighting for women's rights. They travelled the country and Anthony gave speeches demanding that women be given the right to vote. At times, she risked being arrested for sharing her ideas in public.

She was good at strategy and her discipline, energy, and ability to organize made her a strong and successful leader. Anthony and Stanton co-founded the American Equal Rights Association and in 1868 they became editors of the Association's newspaper, *The Revolution,* which helped to spread the ideas of equality and rights for women. Anthony began to lecture to raise money for publishing the newspaper and to support the suffrage movement and became famous throughout the county. Many people admired her, yet others hated her ideas. The 2 women also formed the National Woman Suffrage Association, to push for a constitutional amendment giving women the right to vote.

In 1872, Anthony was arrested for voting. She was tried and fined $100 for her crime. This made many people angry and brought national attention to the suffrage movement.

Anthony spent her life working for women's rights. In 1888, she helped to merge the two largest suffrage associations into one – the National American Women's Suffrage Association. She led the group until 1900, travelling around the country giving speeches, gathering thousands of signatures on petitions, and lobbying Congress every year for women. Anthony died in 1906, 14 years before women were given the right to vote with the passage of the 19th Amendment in 1920.

There shall never be another season of silence
until women
have the same rights as men
Susan B Anthony

"Let go of who you think you're supposed to be; embrace who you are."

Brené Brown (born November 1965) is an American professor, lecturer, author and podcast host.

Brown has spent decades studying the topics of courage, vulnerability, shame, and empathy. She is the author of five number-one *New York Times* bestsellers, namely *The Gifts of Imperfection, Daring Greatly, Rising Strong, Braving the Wilderness,* and *Dare to Lead*. Brené hosts the *Unlocking Us* and *Dare to Lead* podcasts. Her TED talk, "The Power of Vulnerability," is one of the most viewed TED talks of all times. Her filmed lecture, *Brené Brown: The Call to Courage*, debuted on Netflix in 2019.

Born on November 18, 1965, in San Antonio, Texas, she is the oldest of four children. She completed a Bachelor of Social Work degree at the University of Texas at Austin in 1995 – followed by a Master of Social Work degree in 1996 and a Doctor of Philosophy degree in social work at the University of Houston in 2002.

Although Brené Brown inspires everybody, she shouts loudly for women. The very first study she ever did was on the subject of women and shame. At the end of each interview and after hearing the pain that women held around the shame they felt, she made a commitment to ensure that these words and findings reached millions in a meaningful way – resonating with all and allowing people to teach their sons and daughters a better way. According to Brown's extensive research, the antidote to crippling shame is vulnerability. She wants people who tend to think of vulnerability as weakness to change their perceptions and think of it instead as the highest form of courage. She encourages people to admit fear and pain, to reach out to others for help, and to stop believing that keeping our mouths shut and soldiering on is the way that we have to behave in order to be socially acceptable. Her belief is that through this engagement with others, showing vulnerability and making human connections we can live "wholeheartedly." The willingness to be vulnerable and the rejection of socially produced shame will counteract the belief that our vulnerabilities – and therefore ourselves as a whole – are not worthy of love. What an amazing foundation she has laid with her groundbreaking and widespread ideas and research – definitely a woman making HERstory in her plight to break down the conditioned patterns of behaviour that we all hold intrinsically.

Brené considers herself a feminist and has been quoted as saying "I have trouble figuring out why everyone doesn't identify as a feminist. I think expectations and messages around gender and who we are, what we're worth, and what we can do, fuel shame. I don't know how you can be a shame researcher and not be a feminist. I don't know how you can breathe and not be a feminist. You know why I'm a feminist? Because I believe in people's inherent worth – men and women – and that's why I'm a feminist."

Wise words from a wise and incredibly inspirational woman.

let go of who
you think you're
supposed to be
and embrace
who
you
are
Brené Brown

"In her heart she is a mourner for those who have not survived.
In her soul she is a warrior for those who are now as she was then.
In her life she is both celebrant and proof of women's capacity
and will to survive, to become, to act, to change self and society.
And each year she is stronger and there are more of her."

Andrea Rita Dworkin (1946 – 2005) was an American radical feminist activist and writer. She is best known for her analysis of pornography, although her feminist writings, beginning in 1974, span 40 years. They are found in a dozen solo works: nine books of non-fiction, two novels, and a collection of short stories – possibly her most well-known is *Pornography: Men Possessing Women* (1981).

Addressing an anti-sexist men's organisation in 1983, in an acclaimed speech, she said: "The power exercised by men, day to day, in life is power that is institutionalised. It is protected by law. It is protected by religion and religious practice. It is protected by universities, which are strongholds of male supremacy. It is protected by a police force. Against that power, we have silence."

Many articles written about her claimed that Dworkin personified hate. The media often said she hated men, hated sex and hated sexual freedom. In 1998, a writer in the *London Review of Books* saw fit to give his view on her appearance ("overweight and ugly") and how her "frustration" at not having enough sex "has turned her into a man-hater."

When asked how she did the work she did and stayed sane, she replied: "I keep the stories of the women in my heart."

She was motivated by an innate desire to rid the world of pain and oppression.

In the early 1970s, Dworkin spoke of her own experiences of sexual abuse and violence at a time when few did, and always said that until women at the "bottom of the pile" were liberated, none of us could be.

Dworkin would never be silenced and once said: "Women will come back to feminism, because things are going to get far, far worse for us before they get better."

Andrea Dworkin
In her life she
is the proof of
woman's capacity
and will to
survive

"A religion without a Goddess is halfway to atheism."

Dion Fortune (1890 – 1946) was a British occultist, ceremonial magician, novelist and author. She was a co-founder of the Fraternity of the Inner Light, an occult organisation that promoted philosophies which she claimed had been taught to her by spiritual entities known as the Ascended Masters.

She was born Violet Mary Firth in Llandudno, North Wales on 6th December. Her interest in occultism was sparked in 1916, but becoming discontented with the performance of existing organisations, she set about founding her own esoteric group. This group was based in an old officer's mess hut erected at the foot of Glastonbury Tor, named Chalice Orchard – the first headquarters of the Community (later Fraternity and then Society) of the Inner Light. Soon afterward they also acquired a house in the Bayswater district of London which was big enough to accommodate some members, as well as office facilities and a magical lodge.

Working in trance mediumship, Dion Fortune made contacts with certain inner plane adepts, or Masters, whose influence on the Western Esoteric Tradition is still vital to this day.

During this period Dion Fortune wrote several esoteric novels to illustrate the possible practical application of the content of her textbooks and articles in her house journal, the *Inner Light Magazine*.

During the 2nd World War, she organised her own contribution to the war effort on a magical level, with an extended meditation group. They continued to operate in the midst of the Blitz despite a bomb bringing down the roof of her headquarters in 1940. This period was well covered by a series of weekly and then monthly letters to students, later published as *Dion Fortune's Magical Battle of Britain*.

In early January 1946 Dion Fortune returned from Glastonbury feeling tired and unwell, was admitted to Middlesex Hospital in London and died a few days later from leukaemia, at the comparatively young age of 55. She is buried in the municipal cemetery at Glastonbury, with the remains of her close friend and colleague Charles Thomas Loveday close by.

The Society of the Inner Light (the name was changed for legal reasons) continued to operate in much the same way for some years after Dion Fortune's death and continues today as an initiatory school with much the same principles as those upon which it was originally founded.

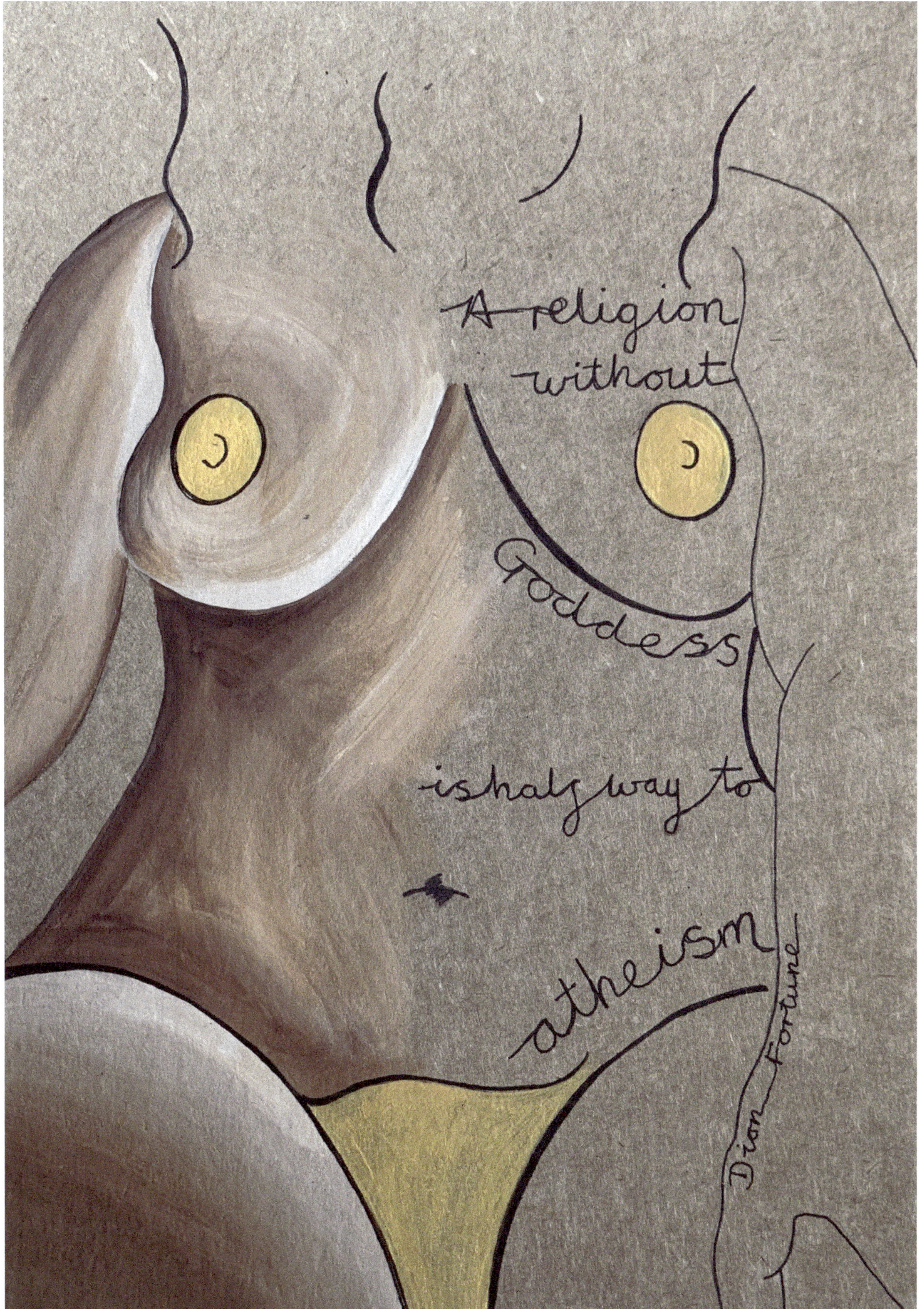

A religion
without
Goddess
is half way to
atheism
Dion Fortune

**"And then all that has divided us will merge.
And then compassion will be wedded to power."**

Judy Chicago (born 20th July 1939) is an American feminist artist, art educator, and writer known for her large collaborative art installation pieces about birth and creation images, which examine the role of women in history and culture.

Born in Chicago, she now lives and works in New Mexico. Her career spans five decades. Chicago studied at the University of California, Los Angeles, graduating with a Master's Degree in painting and sculpture in 1964. In 1970, she launched the first feminist art programme at the California State University, Fresno. At the same time, Chicago dropped her birth name in favour of her birthplace, as a gesture of breaking away from the patriarchal tradition of a woman taking their father's or husband's name.

Chicago's unifying goal is to make a place for female-centred imagery and to overcome the erasure of women's achievements in art and society. Chicago's most influential work, and a milestone in twentieth-century art, is the iconic installation *The Dinner Party 1974–79*, consisting of a large-scale triangular table complete with intricate table settings each laid for a different woman in history – which today is a permanent exhibition housed at the Elizabeth A. Sackler Center for Feminist Art at the Brooklyn Museum.

Judy Chicago is considered one of the most prominent voices in the ongoing dialogue about women and art. She consistently challenges the male-dominated art world, seeking to draw attention to traditionally dismissed crafts, such as needlework and ceramics. She says: "I am trying to make art that relates to the deepest and most mythic concerns of human kind and I believe that, at this moment of history, feminism is humanism."

Some other Judy Chicago quotes I love are:

"…female deities were gradually overshadowed by or incorporated into the attributes of a number of male gods, then eclipsed by the ascendence of the single male deity that now dominates."

"Historically, women have either been excluded from the process of creating the definitions of what is considered art or allowed to participate only if we accept and work within existing mainstream designations. If women have no real role as women in the process of defining art, then we are essentially prevented from helping to shape cultural symbols."

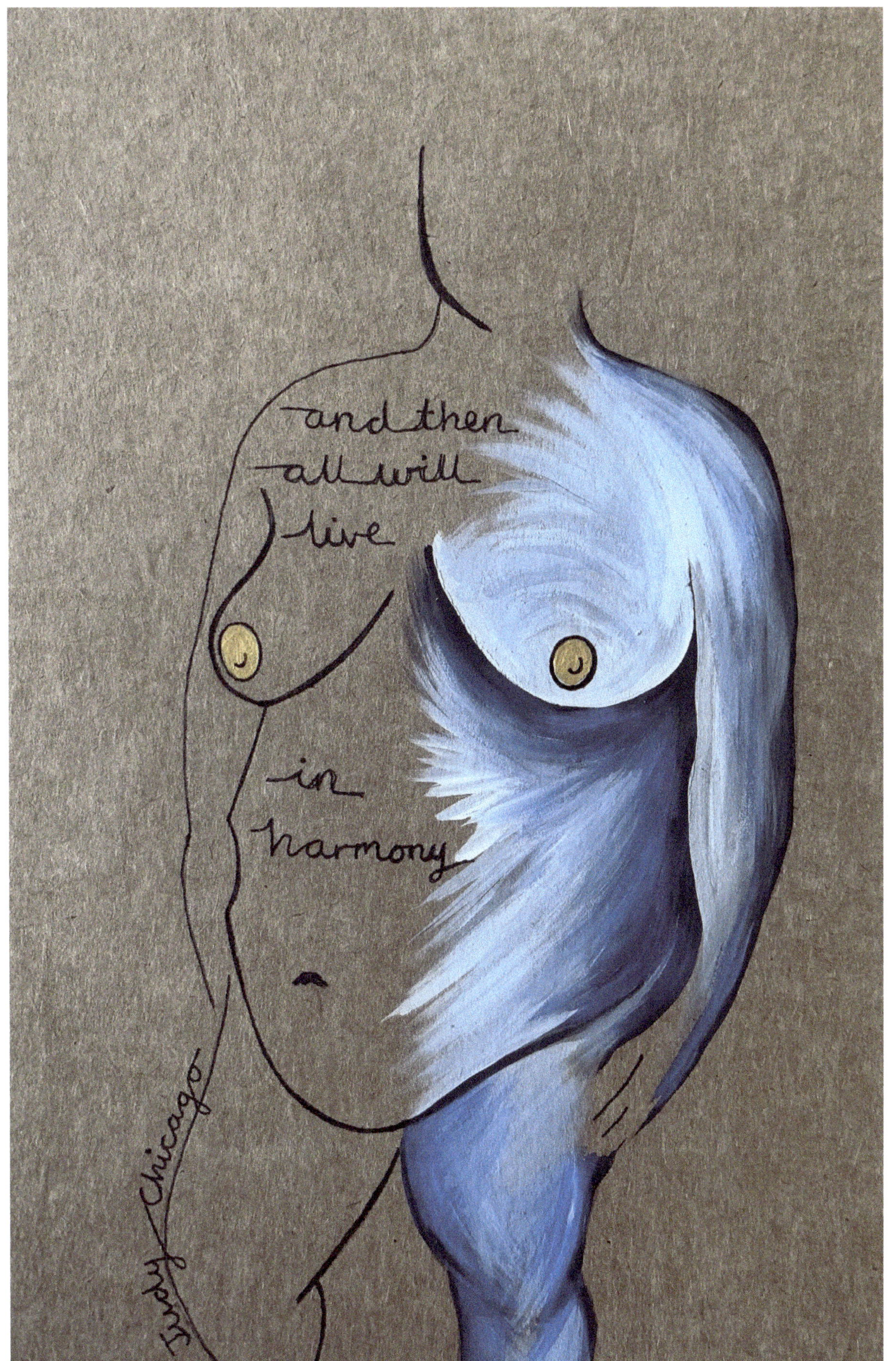

and then
all will
live
in
harmony
Judy Chicago

*"**Every great dream begins with a dreamer.**"*

Known as the "Moses of her people," **Harriet Tubman** (1820 – 1913) was enslaved, escaped, and helped others gain their freedom as a "conductor" of the Underground Railroad. Tubman also served as a scout, spy, guerrilla soldier, and nurse for the Union Army during the Civil War. She is considered the first African American woman to serve in the military.

Tubman's exact birth date is unknown but estimates place it between 1820 and 1822 in Dorchester County, Maryland. Born Araminta Ross, the daughter of Harriet Green and Benjamin Ross, Tubman had eight siblings. By age five, Tubman's owners rented her out to neighbours as a domestic servant. Early signs of her resistance to slavery and its abuses came at age twelve when she intervened to keep her master from beating an enslaved man who tried to escape. She was hit in the head with a two-pound weight, leaving her with a lifetime of severe headaches and narcolepsy.

Although slaves were not legally allowed to marry, Tubman entered a marital union with John Tubman, a free black man, in 1844. She took his name and dubbed herself Harriet.

Contrary to legend, Tubman did not create the Underground Railroad; it was established in the late eighteenth century by black and white abolitionists. Tubman likely benefitted from this network of escape routes and safe houses in 1849, when she and two brothers escaped north. Her husband refused to join her, and by 1851 he had married a free black woman. Tubman returned to the South several times and helped dozens of people escape. Her success led slaveowners to post a $40,000 reward for her capture or death.

Tubman was never caught, never lost a "passenger," and participated in other antislavery efforts. Through the Underground Railroad, Tubman learned the towns and transportation routes characterizing the South – information that made her important to Union military commanders during the Civil War. As a Union spy and scout, Tubman often transformed herself into an aging woman. She would wander the streets under Confederate control and learn from the enslaved population about Confederate troop placements and supply lines. Tubman helped many of these individuals find food, shelter, and even jobs in the North. She also became a respected guerrilla operative.

As a nurse, Tubman dispensed herbal remedies to Black and white soldiers dying from infection and disease.

After the war, Tubman raised funds to aid freedmen. She joined Elizabeth Cady Stanton and Susan B. Anthony in their quest for women's suffrage, cared for her aging parents, and worked with white writer Sarah Bradford on her autobiography as a potential source of income. She married Union soldier Nelson Davis, also born into slavery, who was more than twenty years her junior. Residing in Auburn, New York, she cared for the elderly in her home. In 1874, the Davises adopted a daughter. After an extensive campaign for a military pension, she was finally awarded $8 per month in 1895 as Davis's widow (he died in 1888). In 1899, she was awarded an additional $20 per month for her service. In 1896, she established the Harriet Tubman Home for the Aged, on land near her home. Tubman died in 1913 and was buried with military honours at Fort Hill Cemetery in Auburn, New York.

Every
Great
Dream
Harriet Tubman
begins with a
dreamer

"When the heart is right, the mind and the body will follow."

Although best known for being the wife of famed civil rights leader Dr. Martin Luther King Jr., **Coretta Scott King** (1927 – 2006) created her own legacy in the movement to end injustice. She also worked to continue her husband's legacy after his death.

Coretta Scott was born in Marion, Alabama on April 27th. King's parents were both entrepreneurs and her mother was musically talented. As a child, King expressed interest in music and quickly excelled in grade school as lead in the choir. She was the valedictorian in high school and went on to receive her BA in music from Antioch College in Yellow Springs, Ohio. King was awarded a scholarship to further her music studies at the New England Conservatory of Music in Boston, Massachusetts. While studying at the school King was introduced to doctoral student Martin Luther King Jr. Although she was not initially attracted to him, the two began to date, and married in 1953.

One year later King graduated from the Conservatory of Music and the couple moved to Montgomery, Alabama. Martin took a position as the pastor of Dexter Avenue Baptist Church and the church became a centre for the Civil Rights Movement in Alabama – and eventually the country. Due to her family's participation in the movement King often received death threats. As a result, the couple's house was a continuous target for white supremacist groups.

Throughout her marriage, King appeared side-by-side with her husband fighting against injustice. She also openly criticized the movement's exclusion of women. The Kings had four children – and often, when Martin was travelling, Coretta remained at home, managing a full household on her own.

Dr. Martin Luther King Jr. was assassinated on April 4th, 1968 in Memphis, Tennessee. Coretta Scott King continued to support several issues; openly expressed disdain for the Vietnam War; supported several women's right causes; and travelled internationally, lecturing about racism and economic issues. In 1969, King was awarded the Universal Love Award and became the first non-Italian to hold the distinction. She established the King Center, a memorial which focused on protecting and advancing her husband's legacy.

Coretta Scott King died on January 30th, 2006 from complications of ovarian cancer. Her funeral was attended by several presidents and heads of states who expressed their sadness in losing another prominent figure in the fight for equality. She is buried alongside her husband in Atlanta, Georgia.

when your heart is right

your mind
and body
will follow

Corella Scott King

**"I don't want to get to the end of my life and realise I lived just the length of it.
I want to have lived the width of it as well."**

Diane Ackerman (born 7th October 1948) is an American poet, essayist and author with 24 highly acclaimed published books which are loved by many. She is a naturalist known for her wide-ranging curiosity and poetic explorations of the natural world.

Her essays have appeared in *The New York Times, Smithsonian, Parade, The New Yorker, National Geographic*, and many other journals. Her many books include *New York Times* bestsellers *The Zookeeper's Wife, A Natural History of the Senses, The Human Age*, Pulitzer Prize Finalist, *One Hundred Names for Love*, and even a children's book of poems about the senses of animals.

Her first book was a collection of scientifically accurate poems based on the planets called *The Planets: A Cosmic Pastoral*, as she was fascinated by the little knowledge about them at the time and wanted to learn more (around 1973). At the time, she was a Ph.D. student at Cornell and knew she wanted to work with the arts and sciences, but didn't want to be a scientist. She felt that the universe wasn't knowable from only one perspective and wanted to be able to go exploring – following her curiosity in both worlds. This is the reason for her wide variety of fiction and non-fiction books and poems, as Ackerman loved to throw herself into research, her love of the environment, and all of its living creatures. Her inquisitiveness has taken her to many diverse locations, such as Mata Atlantic in Brazil (working with endangered golden lion tamarins), Patagonia (right whales), Hawaii (humpback whales), California (tagging monarch butterflies at their overwintering sites), French Frigate Shoals (monk seals), Torishima Japan (short-tailed albatross), Texas (with Bat Conservation International), the Amazon rainforest, and Antarctica (penguins).

She has been documented as saying and living by the motto: "I don't want to be a passenger in my own life" and her deep thinking and philosophical words make for great, thoughtful books.

About her writing style, Ackerman says: "Well, I write poetry and non-fiction. I write about nature and human nature. And most often about that twilight zone where the two meet and have something they can teach each other. I like that best. We share instincts and emotions with the rest of the natural world. And part of the predicament that we find ourselves in – existentially – is this tragic attempt that we're making to separate ourselves from nature. To exile ourselves from nature. Which is biologically impossible. And yet we pretend that we can do it, as if nature didn't include us somehow."

In 2015, Ackerman's *The Human Age* won the National Outdoor Book Award in the Natural History Literature category and PEN New England's Henry David Thoreau Prize for nature writing. She has also received an Orion Book Award, John Burroughs Nature Award, Visionary Artist Award, Guggenheim Fellowship, Lavan Poetry Prize, honorary doctorate from Kenyon College, among others, as well as being lionized as a Literary Lion by the New York Public Library. Several of her books have been Pulitzer Prize and National Book Circle Critics Award finalists. In 2016, she was elected to the American Academy of Arts & Sciences. She also has the rare distinction of having a molecule named after her – dianeackerone – a pheromone in crocodilians.

There is much more about Diane Ackerman, but I think we can all agree that she has definitely made HERstory!

I don't want
to get to the end
of my life
and realise
I lived just the
length of it
I want to
have also
lived
the width

Diane Ackerman

"How did I find the Goddess? She called me and I listened."

Lydia Ruyle, also known as Ya-Ya, was an 81-year-old crone and matriarch who passed away in March 2016. She was an artist and scholar who had been pursuing Goddess research for decades.

Her Goddess Banners depict sacred images of the Divine Feminine from the many cultures of the world. Since 1995, the icons have become spirit banners, which fly around the globe weaving the sacred energies of the Divine Feminine. Her research into sacred images of women took her around the world. She created and exhibited her art, did workshops and lead women's journeys throughout the U.S. and internationally. Lydia was the author of two books, _Goddesses of the Americas_ was published in 2016 and _Goddess Icons_ was published in 2002.

Lydia simply called Goddess, and she listened. The Goddess asked her to listen, see, touch, learn, laugh, cry and share with art, stories and sacred places of Mother Earth.

Over 30 years ago, Lydia began collecting images of women from art history, which she taught at the University of Northern Colorado. In 2010, the university created the Lydia Ruyle Room of Women's Art to continue Lydia's mission to teach. In March 1987, an art exhibition at the Loveland Museum and Gallery in Loveland, Colorado called "Better Homes & Goddesses" was the first display of Goddess icons, born for National Women's History Month. In 1993, Lydia invited other women to travel to sacred places with Goddess tours in England, Wales, and Cornwall. Since then, over 300 women have joined her to travel in 14 countries.

Lydia made her first Goddess Banners at the age of 60 for an exhibition in 1995 at the Celsus Library in Ephesus, Turkey where the banners flew and spread their energies throughout the month of July. Since then, the banner collection has grown from 18 to over 300. She has used them to empower, teach, and share their stories at sacred sites in 38 countries.

It was when I became familiar with Lydia Ruyle that I first heard the word HERstory, whilst watching a documentary of the same name. _Herstory: The Visionary Life of Lydia Ruyle and the Banners of the Divine Feminine,_ is a 1-hour documentary film that shows the colourful and heart-warming story of Lydia and her banners which spread their herstories all over the world. The film also documents the incredible story of how her worldwide community came together, with less than 2 weeks' notice, to celebrate her, say goodbye, and honour the passing of a matriarch.

Since 1995, the icons have become spirit banners which fly around the globe weaving the sacred energies of the divine feminine in every corner of the world.

how did I
find the
Goddess
she
called
me
and I
listened
Lydia rhyne

**"The best and most beautiful things in the world cannot be seen or even touched —
they must be felt with the heart."**

Undeterred by deafness and blindness, **Helen Keller** (1880 – 1968) rose to become a major 20th century humanitarian, educator and writer. She advocated for the blind and for women's suffrage and co-founded the American Civil Liberties Union.

Born on June 27th in Tuscumbia, Alabama, Keller was the oldest of two daughters of Arthur H. Keller, a farmer, newspaper editor, and Confederate Army veteran – and his second wife Katherine Adams Keller, an educated woman from Memphis. Several months before Helen's second birthday, a serious illness – possibly meningitis or scarlet fever – left her deaf and blind. She had no formal education until age seven, and since she could not speak, she developed a system for communicating with her family by feeling their facial expressions.

Recognizing her daughter's intelligence, Keller's mother sought help from experts, including inventor Alexander Graham Bell, who had become involved with deaf children. Ultimately, she was referred to Anne Sullivan, a graduate of the Perkins School for the Blind, who became Keller's lifelong teacher and mentor. Although Helen initially resisted her, Sullivan persevered. She used touch to teach Keller the alphabet and to make words by spelling them with her finger on Keller's palm. Within a few weeks, Keller caught on. A year later, Sullivan brought Keller to the Perkins School in Boston, where she learned to read Braille and write with a specially made typewriter. Newspapers chronicled her progress.

At fourteen, she went to New York for two years where she improved her speaking ability, and then returned to Massachusetts to attend the Cambridge School for Young Ladies. With Sullivan's tutoring, Keller was admitted to Radcliffe College, graduating in 1904. Sullivan went with her, helping Keller with her studies.

Even before she graduated, Keller published two books, *The Story of My Life* (1902) and *Optimism* (1903), which launched her career as a writer and lecturer.

Sullivan married Harvard instructor and social critic John Macy in 1905, and Keller lived with them. During that time, Keller's political awareness heightened. She supported the suffrage movement, embraced socialism, advocated for the blind, and became a pacifist during World War I. Keller's life story was featured in the 1919 film, Deliverance. In 1920, she joined Jane Addams, Crystal Eastman, and other social activists in founding the American Civil Liberties Union; four years later she became affiliated with the new American Foundation for the Blind.

After Sullivan's death in 1936, Keller continued to lecture internationally with the support of other aides, and she became one of the world's most-admired women. During World War II, she toured military hospitals bringing comfort to soldiers.

Lifelong activist, Keller met several US presidents and was honoured with the Presidential Medal of Freedom in 1964. She also received honorary doctorates from Glasgow, Harvard, and Temple Universities.

the most beautiful things must be felt with the heart

Helen Keller

When she was growing up, **Anne Frank** (1929 – 1945) wanted to be a writer or a journalist. Unfortunately, her life was cut short by persecution during the Holocaust. Although she was unable to witness it, Anne Frank's writing in her diary became one of the most recognized accounts of life for a Jewish family in Europe during World War II.

Annelies Marie Frank was born on June 12th in Frankfurt, Germany. She lived with her older sister Margot and her parents Otto and Edith Frank. In 1933, when Anne was about five years old, Adolf Hitler and the anti-Jewish National Socialist Party seized power. The Franks decided to flee to Amsterdam in the Netherlands in hopes of a better life. Frank quickly settled in her new home and began attending a Dutch school nearby. Although Frank and her family enjoyed the safety of the Netherlands, this changed when Nazi Germany invaded Poland in 1939 and the Second World War began. Less than a year later, Nazis invaded the Netherlands. The Dutch army quickly surrendered, and the Nazi army began enforcing new laws restricting Jewish mobility. Jewish people were no longer allowed to visit non-Jewish places of business and Jewish children had to attend separate Jewish schools. Soon after, all Jews had to start wearing a Star of David on their clothes for identification.

By the summer of 1942, Jewish people in the Netherlands started receiving calls and notices to report to "work" at Camp Westerbork near the German border. Many of them were unaware that Nazi officials were then transporting them to the two major Jewish killing centers, Auschwitz-Birkenau and Sobibor. On July 5, 1942, Frank's sister Margot received a call to report to a labor camp in Germany. Suspicious of the call and fearing for their lives, the Franks decided to go into hiding instead of reporting to the camp. The very next day, the entire family began hiding in the annex behind the office the family owned at Prinsengracht 263. The family soon welcomed four Dutch Jews into the secret attic apartment to escape persecution. The group hid in the "Secret Annex" for two years, while their friends smuggled food and clothing to help keep them safe. Right before they went into hiding, Frank received a diary for her thirteenth birthday. While she was in hiding with her family, she began recording experiences, thoughts, and feelings in her diary. She also wrote short stories and started a novel about her life.

Sadly, the family's hiding place was discovered by the Gestapo on August 4, 1944. The Franks and their four companions were arrested, along with two of the people who helped them hide. They were all sent to camp Westerbork on August 8, 1944 and prepared for transport. On September 4, 1944 they were placed on a train with 1,019 other Jews and transported to Auschwitz in Poland. Once they arrived, the men and women were separated, and Anne and her sister Margot were selected for manual labor because of their age. Over 350 of the people who arrived in the transport with the Franks were immediately taken to the gas chambers and murdered. In late October of 1944, Anne and her sister Margot were transported to another concentration camp in northern Germany called Bergen-Belsen. The living conditions at this camp were also horrific, and many died from starvation or disease. Anne and Margot both contracted typhus and died in March of 1945 – just a few weeks before the British army liberated the camp on April 15. Their mother Edith also died in early January 1945 in the Auschwitz camp.

When the Soviet army liberated Auschwitz on January 27, 1945, their father Otto was the only one from the annex who survived. When he was released, he learned that all of his family was dead. However, he returned to the Netherlands and discovered that his friend Miep Gies was able to preserve Anne Frank's diary before the Nazis raided their hiding place. Otto read his daughters writings and saw that she wanted to become a journalist or a writer, so he published her diary in June of 1947. The book grew in popularity and was later translated into over 70 languages. In 1960, the secret annex where the family hid was turned into a museum called the Anne Frank House.

whoever is
happy
will
make
others
happy
too
Anni Frank

"I just know that something good is going to happen."

Catherine Bush CBE (born 30th July 1958) is an English singer, songwriter, musician, dancer and record producer. In 1978, at age 19, she topped the UK Singles Chart for four weeks with her debut single _Wuthering Heights_. She was the first female artist to achieve a UK number one with a self-written song (which incidentally she claims to have written under the light of the full moon). She was what music sounded like when it was the authentic creation of its author. She was rare.

She has released ten albums across a hugely sporadic career. Among those records are some of the most boundary-pushing, polarising and fascinating pop songs of all time.

One secret of the singer Kate Bush's artistry is that she has never feared the ludicrous – she tries things that other musicians would be too careful or cool to go near. Because of this, she has had an undeniable impact on the landscape of music for female artists. Her innovative and passionately visual songs set the precedent when there was none, and took risks in her work, channelling different characters, going against expectation and speaking her truth however that looked and sounded to her.

On both a lyrical and practical level, Bush laid groundwork for women being able to exist unapologetically in an otherwise male-dominated industry. She demonstrates a stunning versatility in subject matter in a manner that never steers from her central identifiable style. Her music is raw and tender, encapsulating feelings of loss, grief – and simply being allowed to feel. In 2018 she released a book, _How to Be Invisible_, filled with lyrics from her songs – documenting the dynamic nature of the female experience. These lyrics light a fire of hope inside us all – especially when she sings, "I just know that something good is gonna happen" in _Cloudbusting._ She speaks to our desire to feel significant in _Running Up That Hill_ when she sings, "Tell me, we both matter, don't we?" She speaks to a universal desire to be set free from rigid societal expectation in the experimental _Leave It Open_ when she says that "we let the weirdness in."

What makes Kate great is that she is able to be so distinctly personal whilst reaching out and resonating so stunningly with multiple generations of women and making them feel seen. Every emotion is acknowledged, explored and displayed without shame. She strived for individuality and magic, saying: "We have such little mystery in our lives generally because of how we live now. I mean, of course, mystery is all around us, but the way we live our lives now, we're too busy to be bothered with it."

Amongst other accomplishments and a multitude of worldwide nominations, Kate Bush's wins include a Billboard Music Award in 2003 for _This Woman's Work_; a Brit awarded in 1987 for Best British Female; an Edison Music Award in 1979 for Best International Single with _Wuthering Heights_; an Evening Standard Theatre award in 2014 for _Before the Dawn_; Ivor Novello awards in 1979 for outstanding lyrics; best international performer for _Babooshka_ in 1980; outstanding contribution to British music in 2002; an NME award in 1979 for best female singer; a Q songwriter award in 2001 and the Rock and Roll Hall of fame named her best female singer in 1980.

Kate Bush and her work consolidates the idea that women deserve to safely own the space they occupy and the art they create. We thank her for shaping HERstory.

I just know that
something
good
is
going to happen
Kate Bush

**"Be wicked, be brave, be drunk, be reckless, be dissolute, be despotic,
be an anarchist... be anything you like, but for pity's sake
be it to the top of your bent. Live – live fully,
live passionately, live disastrously."**

Victoria Mary Sackville-West (The Honorable Lady Nicolson, CH) (1892 – 1962) was usually known as Vita Sackville-West. She was an English author and garden designer. She was a successful novelist, poet, and journalist, as well as a prolific letter writer and diarist.

Vita was born at Knole Estate, the only daughter to Lionel Edward Sackville-West (later third Baron Sackville) and his cousin, Victoria Sackville-West.

As a young girl, Vita delighted in showing visitors around Knole, and she expressed profound attachment to the estate throughout her life. It was therefore a constant source of distress to her that, as a woman, she was unable to inherit her ancestral home. The Knole Estate was passed to her cousin Eddy after her father's death.

Vita married diplomat Harold Nicolson in 1913. The Nicolsons enjoyed a close relationship and a very successful marriage, later documented in their son Nigel's book, *Portrait of a Marriage* (1973).

Both had affairs with same-sex partners throughout their married life, Vita perhaps most famously with the writer and Bloomsbury group member, Virginia Woolf. Vita and Harold's mutual acceptance of each other's lovers affirmed their commitment to their marriage.

Vita had begun writing novels, plays, and poetry as a girl – but her experiences in Constantinople while she and Harold were in residence prompted her to write *Poems of East and West* in 1917, beginning a long writing career.

Her poem "The Land" (1926) won the Hawthornden prize in 1927. She and Harold purchased Sissinghurst Castle in 1930, a run-down Elizabethan mansion in Kent, and began immediately to renovate both house and garden.

Vita became increasingly reclusive as the Second World War began. She spent her last decades ensconced at Sissinghurst, writing novels and gardening books in its famous tower, and creating the splendour of its gardens.

Vita began speaking for the National Trust in 1928, helped to negotiate the institution's takeover of Knole in the early 1940s, and became, along with Harold, a member of the Trust's council. Sissinghurst became a Trust property upon her death in 1962.

Live life passionately
live life fully
Live life
Vita Sackville

"I would always rather be happy than dignified."

One of the most famous Victorian women writers, and a prolific poet, **Charlotte Brontë** is best known for her novels, including _Jane Eyre_ (1847). Brontë was born on April 21, 1816 in the village of Thornton, West Riding, Yorkshire. Charlotte's mother, Maria Branwell Brontë, died when her daughter was only five years old. Born to a prosperous tea merchant and grocer, Maria Branwell was raised in Penzance, Cornwall, married Patrick Brontë in 1812, and bore six children in seven years – Maria (1813), Elizabeth (1815), Charlotte (1816), Patrick (1817), Emily (1818), and Anne (1820) – and died of cancer at the age of 38.

During Maria Brontë's illness, her sister, Elizabeth Branwell, came from Penzance to care for the family temporarily, but, because Patrick Brontë's attempts to remarry after his wife's death were unsuccessful, she stayed until she died in 1842. Often left to their own devices, the siblings played on the wide expanse of moors that surrounded their parsonage home; they also read voraciously and engaged in the imaginative play that was to develop quickly into literary inventiveness.

In 1824, when she was eight years old, Charlotte and Emily joined their older sisters at the newly opened Clergy Daughters' School at Cowan Bridge in the parish of Tunstall. The aim of the school was to provide a "plain and useful education" that would allow young women "to maintain themselves in the different Stations of Life to which Providence may call them."

Charlotte Brontë's earliest report from school reads: "Reads tolerably – Writes indifferently – understands arithmetic a little – knows nothing of Grammar, Geography or History and sews neatly." Charlotte found the rigors of boarding school life harsh. The food was so badly prepared under unsanitary conditions and many students got ill – one of them being Maria. Patrick Brontë was not informed of his eldest daughter's condition until February 1825, two months after Maria began to show symptoms. When he saw her, he immediately withdrew her from the school and she died at home in early May. Elizabeth, in the meantime, had also fallen ill and she also sadly died in March.

The loss of Elizabeth and Maria profoundly affected Charlotte's life and probably helped shape her personality as well. Suddenly becoming the eldest child in a motherless family forced her into a position of leadership. Patrick Brontë started to tutor his four remaining children at home and they were allowed to choose freely from their father's library.

In December of 1836, Charlotte Brontë decided to try her hand at professional writing, with the hope of earning her living as a publishing poet. She sought the advice of Robert Southey, then poet laureate of England, to whom she sent a selection of her poems. The discouraging response in his letter of March 12, 1837 has become infamous: "Literature cannot be the business of a woman's life: & it ought not to be. The more she is engaged in her proper duties, the less leisure she will have for it, even as an accomplishment and a recreation." Charlotte obviously ignored that advice. Between January 1837 and July 1838, Brontë wrote more than 60 poems and verse fragments, including drafts of what were eventually to be some of her best poetical works. In 1845, she revised them into poems and published them, but after writing and publishing _Jane Eyre,_ she never wrote poetry again. It was the passion and rebellion of _Jane Eyre_ (1847) that earned her fame. When visiting London she moved in the best literary circles. She later published _Shirley_ (1849), written during and after the tragic deaths of her three siblings within a single year. _Shirley_ displayed Charlotte's engagement with both women's rights and radical workers' movements.

In June 1854, she married her father's curate Arthur Nicholls, who had long been a loyal suitor. She became pregnant but died at the young age of 38 on 31 March 1855. Her cause of death varies from tuberculosis to pregnancy complications.

I would
rather be
happy
than dignified
Bronte
Marron

"I just knew that if it could be done, it had to be done, and I did it."

Gertrude Caroline Ederle (1905 – 2003) was an American competition swimmer, Olympic champion, and former world record-holder in five events. Among other nicknames, the press sometimes called her "Queen of the Waves."

On August 6th 1926, on her second attempt, 19-year-old Gertrude Ederle became the first woman to swim the 21 miles from Dover, England, to Cape Griz-Nez across the English Channel, which separates Great Britain from the northwestern tip of France.

Ederle was born to German immigrants on October 23rd in New York City. She did not learn to swim until she was nine years old – and it was not until she was 15 that she learned the proper form in the water. Just two years later, at the 1924 Paris Olympics, Ederle won a gold medal in the 4 x 100-meter relay and a bronze medal in the 100- and 400-meter freestyle races. In June 1925, Ederle became the first woman to swim the length of New York Bay, breaking the previous men's record by swimming from the New York Battery to Sandy Hook, New Jersey, in 7 hours 11 minutes. That same summer, Ederle made her first attempt at crossing the notoriously cold and choppy English Channel, but after eight hours and 46 minutes, her coach, Jabez Wolff, forced her to stop, out of concern that she was swallowing too much saltwater. Ederle disagreed and fired Wolff, replacing him with T.W. Burgess, a skilled Channel swimmer.

On August 6, 1926, Ederle entered the water at Cape Gris-Nez in France at 7:08 a.m. to make her second attempt at the Channel. The water was predictably cold as she started out that morning, but unusually calm. Twice that day, however – at noon and 6 p.m. – Ederle encountered storms along her route and Burgess urged her to end the swim. Ederle's father and sister, though, who were riding in the boat along with Burgess, agreed with Ederle that she should stay the course. Ederle persevered through storms and heavy swells, and, finally, at 9:04 p.m. after 14 hours and 31 minutes in the water, she reached the English coast, becoming the sixth person and first woman to swim the Channel successfully. Furthermore, she had bettered the previous record by two hours.

Afterward, Ederle told Alec Rutherford of *The New York Times*, "I knew it could be done, it had to be done, and I did it."

Ederle damaged her hearing during the Channel swim and went on to spend much of her adult life teaching deaf children in New York City to swim. She died in 2003 at the age of 98.

I just knew that
if it could
be done
it had
to be
done
and I did it
Gertrude Ederle

"I am in a charming state of confusion."

Augusta Ada King Lovelace (1815 – 1852), Countess of Lovelace was an English mathematician and writer, chiefly known for her work on Charles Babbage's proposed mechanical general-purpose computer, the Analytical Engine.

Ada Lovelace, the daughter of poet Lord Byron, has been called "the first computer programmer" for writing an algorithm for a computing machine in the mid-1800s.

Lord Byron's marriage to Lovelace's mother, Lady Anne Isabella Milbanke Byron, was not a happy one. Lady Byron separated from her husband only weeks after their daughter was born. A few months later, Lord Byron left England, and Lovelace never saw her father again. He died in Greece when Ada was 8 years old.

Lovelace had an unusual upbringing for an aristocratic girl in the mid-1800s. At her mother's insistence, tutors taught her mathematics and science. Such challenging subjects were not standard fare for women at the time, but her mother believed that engaging in rigorous studies would prevent Lovelace from developing her father's moody and unpredictable temperament. Lovelace was also forced to lie still for extended periods of time because her mother believed it would help her develop self-control.

Around the age of 17, Ada met Charles Babbage, a mathematician and inventor. The pair became friends, and the much older Babbage served as a mentor to Lovelace. Through Babbage, Lovelace began studying advanced mathematics with University of London professor Augustus de Morgan. Lovelace was fascinated by Babbage's ideas. Known as the father of the computer, he invented the difference engine, which was meant to perform mathematical calculations. Lovelace got a chance to look at the machine before it was finished and was captivated by it. Babbage also created plans for another device known as the analytical engine, designed to handle more complex calculations. Ada added her own thoughts and ideas on the machine. Her notes ended up being three times longer than the original article and her work was published in 1843, in an English science journal. Lovelace used only the initials "A.A.L.," for Augusta Ada Lovelace, in the publication.

In her notes, Lovelace described how codes could be created for the device to handle letters and symbols along with numbers. She also theorized a method for the engine to repeat a series of instructions, a process known as looping that computer programs use today. For her work, Lovelace is often considered to be the first computer programmer.

In 1835, Lovelace married William King, who became the Earl of Lovelace three years later. She then took the title of Countess of Lovelace. They shared a love of horses and had three children together. From most accounts, he supported his wife's academic endeavours.

Lovelace died from uterine cancer in London on November 27, 1852. She was buried next to her father, in the graveyard of the Church of St. Mary Magdalene in Hucknall, England.

In 1980, the U.S. Department of Defense named a newly developed computer language "Ada," after Lovelace.

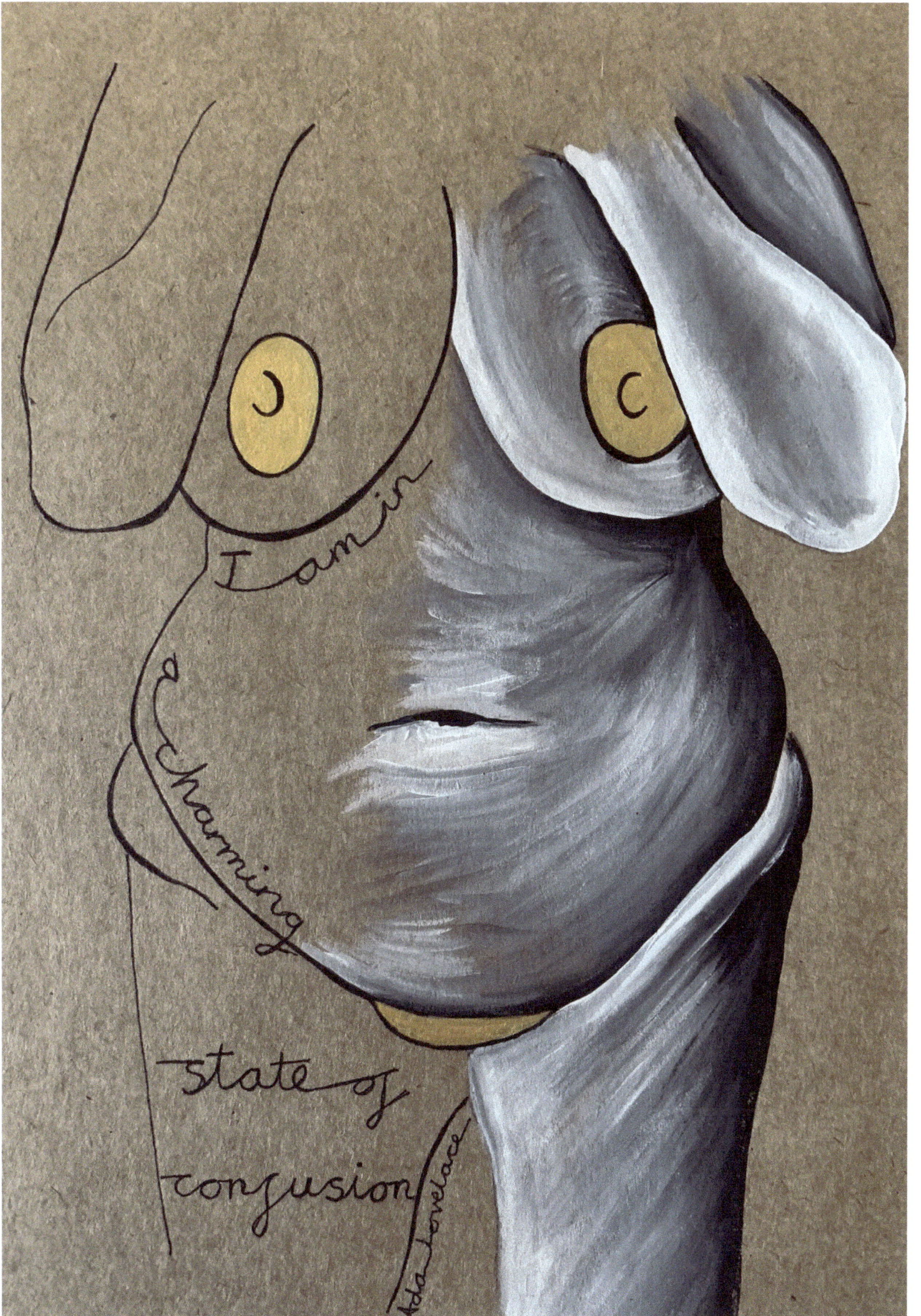

I am in
a charming
state of
confusion
Ada Lovelace

"You have been criticizing yourself for years and it hasn't worked.
Try approving of yourself and see what happens."

Louise Lynn Hay (1926 – 2017) was an American motivational author and the founder of Hay House. She authored several New Thought self-help books, including the 1984 book *You Can Heal Your Life*. I can say with my hand on my heart that this book truly changed my life.

Louise Hay is also known as one of the founders of the self-help movement. Her first book, *Heal Your Body*, was published in 1976, long before it was fashionable to discuss the connection between the mind and body. Revised and expanded in 1988, this best-selling book introduced Louise's concepts to people in 33 different countries and has been translated into 25 languages throughout the world.

Through Louise's healing techniques and positive philosophy, millions have learned how to create more of what they want in their lives – including more wellness in their bodies, minds, and spirits. Her own personal philosophy was forged from her tormented upbringing. Her childhood was unstable and impoverished, and her teen years were marked by abuse. Louise ran away from home and ended up in New York City, where she became a model and married a prosperous businessman. Although it appeared that her life had turned around, it was not until the marriage ended 14 years later that her healing really began.

Louise started what would become her life's work in New York City in 1970. She attended meetings at the Church of Religious Science and began training in the ministerial program. She became a popular speaker at the church, and soon found herself counselling clients. This work quickly blossomed into a full-time career. After several years, Louise compiled a reference guide detailing the mental causes of physical ailments and developed positive thought patterns for reversing illness and creating health.
She began traveling throughout the United States, lecturing and facilitating workshops.

Louise was able to put her philosophies into practice when she was diagnosed with cancer. She considered the alternatives to surgery and drugs, and instead developed an intensive program of affirmations, visualization, nutritional cleansing, and psychotherapy. Within six months, she was completely healed of cancer.

In 1980, Louise moved back to her native Southern California, and began putting her workshop methods on paper. In 1984, *You Can Heal Your Life* was published. In it, Louise explains how our beliefs and ideas about ourselves are often the cause of our emotional problems and physical maladies – and how, by using certain tools, we can change our thinking and our lives for the better.

You Can Heal Your Life reached the *New York Times* bestseller list and remained on it for 13 consecutive weeks. More than 50 million copies of *You Can Heal Your Life* have been sold throughout the world. Twenty years later, due to her appearances on the *Oprah Winfrey Show, You Can Heal Your Life* was again on the *New York Times* bestseller list – the first time in history that has happened!

In 1985, Louise began her famous support group, "The Hayride," with six men diagnosed with AIDS. By 1988, the group had grown to a weekly gathering of 800 people and had moved to an auditorium in West Hollywood. Once again, Louise had started a movement of love and support long before people began to wear red ribbons in their lapels.

Louise started Hay House, Inc., a successful publishing company. What began as a small venture in the living room of her home has turned into a prosperous corporation that has sold millions of books and products worldwide. In addition, The Hay Foundation is a non-profit organization that encourages and financially supports diverse organizations that supply food, shelter, counselling, hospice care and money to those with AIDS, battered women and other crises. The foundation will continue the good work that Louise began over 30 years ago. Louise transitioned on August 30, 2017 in San Diego, CA at the age of 90.

51

you have been criticising yourself for years and it hasn't worked

try approving of yourself and see what happens.

Louise Hay

Nat Shaw Artist

**"My mother told me to be a lady.
And for her, that meant be your own person, be independent."**

Despite her diminutive stature, **Justice Ruth Bader Ginsburg** was a towering force to be reckoned with. She was the second woman to ascend to the US Supreme Court in 1993 and fought tirelessly to give a voice to the voiceless – speaking up for women, minorities, and the LGBTQ community. Notoriously known as RBG, she became the face of Democratic feminism at 85, as she consistently and courageously stood her ground in the face of sexism.

When studying at Harvard Law School in 1957, she was one of just nine female undergraduates among a group of 500 men and suffered countless indignities. The women were refused access to the library (the same fate that befell Virginia Woolf at Cambridge decades earlier); they were not called upon in class; and were asked by the dean to explain, one by one, why they had enrolled at the university and taken a place from a man. Confronted with this onslaught of injustices, Ginsburg knew how to play the game, and hid her ambition in order to progress. To the latter insult she speciously explained that she was getting a degree to be a more empathetic wife to her husband Marty, a second-year student at Harvard Law.

Although she was a full-time caregiver to her one-year-old daughter and cancer-patient spouse, Ginsburg graduated valedictorian when she transferred to Columbia. In her career, Ruth Bader Ginsburg was unconquerable. She persevered when men tried to hold her back and went on to change the world for the better – as evidenced by her early cases, which sought access to reproductive healthcare, pregnancy benefits and equal pay. Ginsburg was determined to secure women's rights, but also strived to overturn civil rights violations, no matter who they affected. For example, the Justice used her platform to grant the disabled state-funded support in their communities (1999) and legalise gay marriage in all 50 states (2015).

Ruth Bader Ginsburg showed how the patriarchy negatively impacts men and women and her pro-women, pro-immigration and pro-minority verdicts just proved that she chipped away at the glass ceiling within the legal system, breaking conventions and making a future for female representation within the justice system. She hoped that there will be a time when all nine Supreme Court Justices are women. She was quoted as saying: "People are shocked [when I say that] but there have been nine men and nobody's ever raised a question about that."

RBG realized that women could never achieve equality with men if outdated stereotypes were holding them back. She challenged law after law where women and men were provided different rights due to gender stereotypes. One such law gave men preference in being chosen to administer estates (men were more familiar with money and business). Another example was a Social Security law that deprived men of receiving benefits from a deceased wife (wives were typically only secondary breadwinners).

Ginsburg's appreciation for gender equality extended to her home life. She and husband, Martin Ginsburg had an equality in their marriage that was almost unheard of in the 1950s. Martin, who she met on a blind date while an undergraduate at Cornell and married in 1954, was committed to sharing the child-rearing and housework. He is rumoured to have taken on the majority of the household's cooking. He left a lucrative law career in New York to move with her to Washington, when President Jimmy Carter named Ginsburg to the United States Court of Appeals for the District of Columbia Circuit. Without the support of an equal marriage, it's unlikely Ginsburg could have achieved all that she did.

RBG definitely moved the bar forward on equal rights. As much as for what she accomplished, Ginsburg will be remembered for how she accomplished it. She saw inequities and chipped away at them for more than half a century. She never gave up. She just kept fighting. The combination of her tenacity and her intellectual acuity made her someone who could not be ignored.

my mother told
me to be
a lady
and for
her that
meant
be your
own person
—
be independent
Justice Ruth Bader Ginsburg

"I am mine before I am anyone else's."

Nayyirah Waheed is a poet and author who has published two books of poetry. Women all over the world resonate with her life-changing words. Waheed is a reclusive writer who doesn't reveal many details about her life, and her poetry is known for being short, minimalistic and incredibly touching, covering topics such as love, identity, race, and feminism.

Not much is known about Waheed's background and childhood. Waheed describes herself as a "quiet poet" who doesn't share much about her life. What is known is that Waheed began writing at the age of eleven after being assigned to write a poem for a community newspaper by her English teacher. Since then, she has published two books and gained a loyal following.

I decided to include Nayyirah Waheed as a woman making HERstory because she is current and changing the way that women think and feel about themselves with her words. In this modern age, social media is the tool that younger generations understand – not only how they connect and interact, but also how they get their cues, prompts and identity on how to behave and what is "expected" of them in today's society. To be drowning in air brushed images, photoshopped perfection, and everybody sharing their "perfect and mostly unattainable" lives – and then to be thrown a life raft in the shape of a Waheed poem or inspirational quote, is not only life-affirming, but monumentally life-changing. This is the double-edged sword of social media, as Nayyirah Waheed's audience is mainly online.

Words such as "I am mine before I am anyone else's", "I have always been the woman of my dreams", "When I am afraid to speak is when I speak. That is when it is most important" and "You not wanting me was the beginning of me wanting myself. Thank you" are simply written with a typewriter onto a white background, but are shared thousands of times daily to uplift people all over the world, and her impact is huge.

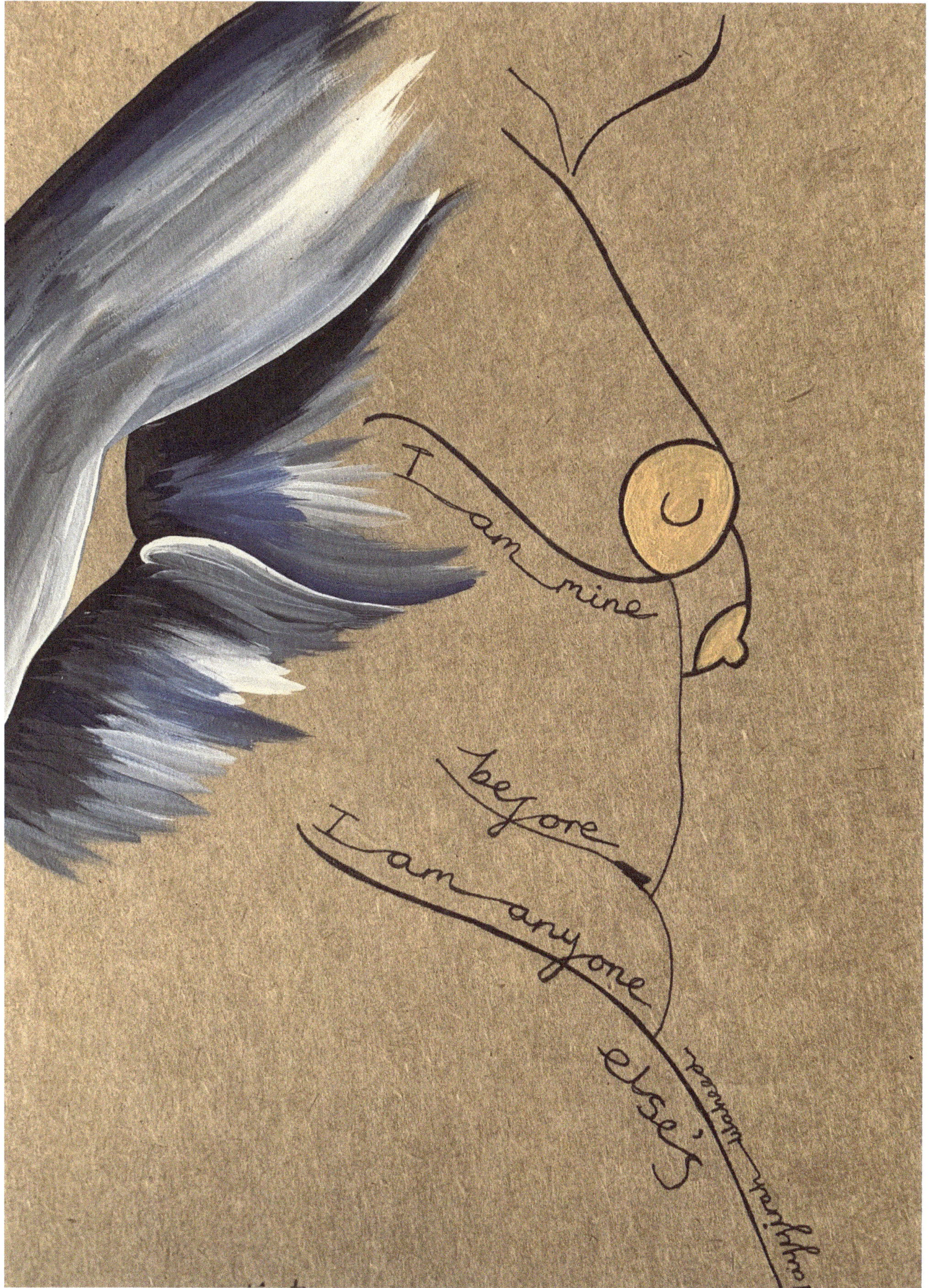

I am mine
before
I am anyone
else's

"I found myself, I made myself and I said what I had to say."

Over a century ago, **Suzanne Valadon** began painting lively nude portraits of sensual and self-assured women, with full, curvy bodies and pubic hair. Occasionally, she painted nude men as well, bucking art's historical tradition and presenting them as figures of desire. Her canvases were full of bold outlines, vibrant colours and loose brushwork – and she deftly illustrated her subjects' interior lives, rather than the idealized scenes of leisure so prevalent at the time. Championed by some of her most famous contemporaries, including Edgar Degas and Pierre-Auguste Renoir, Valadon was no minor artist, and one of the few women painters of the era to receive critical acclaim. Yet, like many women artists of the 20th century, her fame faded after her death.

From the start, Valadon was a controversial figure in Paris' thriving art scene at the turn of the century, known as much for her bohemian attitudes and provocative personal life as her distinct, rebellious vision.

Suzanne Valadon was born Marie-Clémentine Valadon to an impoverished single mother in Montmartre in 1865. She was a headstrong, imaginative child who exasperated the nuns trying to teach her. Valadon held a series of short-lived menial jobs before training as a circus performer at 15 years old, but her career was cut short by a back injury sustained during a trapeze stunt. It was during her recovery that Valadon began to draw. Lacking the training or money typically needed to enter the art world, she began modelling for artists. It was a salacious job, considered to be on par with sex work at the time, but one that offered her direct access to the art milieu of Paris.

Her reputation spread through word of mouth, as well as her determination to socialize and network in spaces exclusive to male artists, particularly the smoky, absinthe-steeped rooms of Parisian cafe culture. Soon Valadon was populating the works of some of the most famous Impressionist painters of the time. Most famously, she danced across Renoir's scenes. But Valadon did more than just pose. She used the sessions as informal training, observing and learning from the artists for whom she modelled.
She began to stake her claim in the art world while raising a young child, having become pregnant at 18. She didn't start to receive attention for her work until her late 20s.

When she married businessman Paul Mousis and moved out of Paris, her artistic output slowed. Further complicating her life were her son Maurice's troubles in school, and his growing alcohol addiction, which first took hold when he was a teenager. She often put her energy into Maurice's artistic talent, hoping that a painting practice would ease his troubles. She didn't give her full attention to her art career again until she was 45 years old, after she left her husband for the younger artist André Utter. She began to paint prolifically, making studies of herself and her family, as well as the nudes she became known for. In 1909, her painting "Summer" was accepted into the new and trendy Salon d'Automne, followed by her first solo show in 1911 where her nudes were described as "powerful," and that they "enchant the viewer by virtue of the truth that emanates from them."

Valadon's figures didn't adhere to the delicate femininity that was expected of the time. They were contemporary women with modern clothes and hairstyles, as well as body hair – a far cry from the timeless nudes so prevalent in art history. Even more surprising were Valadon's depictions of nude men, though she rarely painted them. The fact she was painting male nudes at all in the early 20th century was deemed pretty shocking! Valadon also chronicled her own body as she aged, painting herself nude well into her 60s – which, at the time raised a few eyebrows!

In the last decade of her career, Valadon exhibited worldwide, with shows in New York, Prague, Chicago and Berlin. In 1938, she died at the age of 72 after suffering a stroke. At the time, French art critic George Besson called her "the most justifiably famous" woman painter of the era.

54

Suzanne Valadon

I made
myself

I found myself

and I said what I had to say

"I stand on the sacrifices of a million women before me."

Rupi Kaur (born 4 October 1992) is an Indian-born Canadian poet, illustrator, and author – and she is my ultimate favourite and a huge influence in my life.

She received widespread popularity after the publication of her debut book *Milk and Honey* (2014), which went on to sell over 3 million copies worldwide and spent more than a year on *The New York Times Best Seller* list. In 2017, Kaur released her second book, *The Sun and Her Flowers*, leading her to be named on the BBC's 100 Women in 2017. Her third poetry collection, *home body*, was released on Nov. 17, 2020.

Her work explores relationships, the immigrant experience, love, loss and sexual trauma.

Rupi Kaur was born into a Sikh family in Punjab, India. She immigrated to Canada with her parents when she was four years old. Her father worked as a truck driver and her family eventually settled in Brampton. She was inspired by her mother to draw and paint and she continued her art into her teens, but at age seventeen, she shifted her focus to writing and performing.

In March 2015, Kaur posted a series of photographs to Instagram depicting herself with menstrual blood stains on her clothing and bed sheets. Described as a piece of visual poetry, it is considered among her more notable works, challenging the prevalent societal menstrual taboos. However, those photos were pulled down for not complying with the site's terms of service. Instagram brought back the images, citing a mistaken removal, and apologized to her after being criticized for displaying the very response that the works were intended to critique.

As in Gurmukhi script, her work is written exclusively in lowercase, using only the period as a form of punctuation. Rupi writes this way to honour her culture. She said that she enjoys the equality of letters and that the style reflects her worldview. Her written work is meant to be an experience that is easy for the reader to follow, with simple drawings to elevate her words.

i stand on
the sacrifices
of a
million
women before me

Rupi Kaur

Kat Shaw prides herself on breaking through the stereotypical views of beauty that have been cast upon society by the media, having made her name painting the glorious reality that is a woman's body.

Her nude studies of real women garnered unprecedented popularity within only a few short months, as women were crying out for themselves to be portrayed in art, rather than the airbrushed images of the perfection of the female form that are so rife in today's culture.

After graduating with a fine art degree, Kat achieved a successful full-time teaching career for 14 years and continues to teach art part-time whilst passionately pursuing her mission of world domination by empowering as many women as possible to reach their fullest potential by embracing their bodies and loving themselves wholeheartedly.

Kat spreads her inspirational magic through her artwork, her Wellbeing business, "Fabulously Imperfect," and her dedication to Goddess energy.

Reiki is a huge part of her life, and as a Reiki Master, Kat is committed to sharing Reiki, teaching Usui, Angelic and Karuna Reiki, and channelling Reiki energy through her artwork to uplift and heal.

As a Sister of Avalon, Kat also works directly with her Goddess consciousness, connecting to Goddess and Priestess energy and translating it into Divine Feminine infused paintings to inspire women and spread Goddess love.

Kat is also a bellydancer and an avid pioneer to improve the lives of rescue animals, and mum to a gorgeous teenage daughter.

Prints, canvasses, cards, original paintings and merchandise are also available at the KatShawArtist Etsy shop: Www.Etsy.com/uk/shop/KatShawArtist

The AMAZING Kat Shaw!

Acknowledgements

A deep bow to ALL the magnificent women who have walked before us and changed our world for the better.

Thank you to all of the glorious Goddesses who allowed me to honour their bodies by painting them – may we all make HERstory as we spread empowerment to every woman.

Heartfelt gratitude to Trista Hendren who made my dream come true by making this book a reality.

Upcoming Books

Kali Rising: Holy Rage – Edited by C. Ara Campbell, Jaclyn Cherie, Trista Hendren, and Pat Daly

Women's Sovereignty and Body Autonomy Beyond Roe v. Wade – Edited by Trista Hendren, Arlene Bailey, Sharon Smith, and Pat Daly

A Poiesis of the Creative Cosmos: Celebrating Her within PaGaian Sacred Ceremony – Glenys Livingstone, Ph.D.

Somatic Shamanism: Your Fleshy Knowing as the Tree of Life – Kay Louise Aldred

Embodied Education: Creating Safe Space for Learning, Facilitating and Sharing – Kay Louise Aldred and Dan Aldred

Pain Perspectives: Finding Meaning in the Fire – Edited by Kay Louise Aldred, Trista Hendren, and Pat Daly

Goddess Chants and Songs Book – Edited by Trista Hendren, Anique Radiant Heart, and Pat Daly

Heart to Heart: Words from Goddess/Divine Feminine Wisdom – Kat Shaw
Imperfectly Fabulous – Kat Shaw

Out of Darkness She Speaks – Leonor Murciano-Luna, PhD

Anthologies and children's books on the Black Madonna, Mary Magdalene, Mother Mary, Cerridwen, Aradia, Kali, Brigid, Sophia, Spider Woman, Persephone, The Old Antlered One/Ancient Deer Goddess, An' Cailleach and Hecate are also in the works. Details to be announced.

http://thegirlgod.com/publishing.php

www.ingramcontent.com/pod-product-compliance
Lightning Source LLC
LaVergne TN
LVHW071449180726
843512LV00018B/1329